Capelle on 9-Ball
Archer vs. Reyes

Johnny Archer vs.
Efren Reyes
Sands Regency Open 23,
June, 1996

Philip B. Capelle

Billiards Press
Huntington Beach, CA

Capelle on 9-Ball
Archer vs. Reyes

Publication Date: November, 2002
Copyright © 2002 by Phil Capelle
Published by: Billiards Press
　　　　　　　P.O. Box 400
　　　　　　　Midway City, CA 92655

First Printing

Printed in the United Stated of America

10　9　8　7　6　5　4　3　2　1

Library of Congress Control Number
2002094339

ISBN　0-9649204-4-1

Dedication

This book is dedicated to Johnny Archer and Efren Reyes, whose immense talents came together to produce a most memorable match, and to Pat Fleming and the people at Accu-Stats Video Productions.

Acknowledgements

One of the great joys of working on books is the ideas and enthusiasm I get from friends and those who work with me on the projects. I was showing an early draft to long time friend Paul Gray when he provided me with the spark that led to a complete new perspective on the project. What was to be a brief overview of the match turned into a serious research project.

Paul Harris, who has worked with me on previous projects, once again was the man at the computer drawing the diagrams, laying out the book and providing the cover art.

I appreciated the support of Tom Shaw and my friends at *Pool & Billiard Magazine*. Todd Fleitman provided numerous suggestions for improving the text and for insuring the accuracy of the illustrations. Wayne Whiting also was kind enough to proof read the text.

Thanks also go to Johnny Archer and Efren Reyes, who played such an exciting and memorable match. Bill Incardona and Dace Maddox are also to be applauded for their insights into the pro game.

Pat Fleming of Accu-Stats Video Productions, who filmed and produced the match, was extremely supportive of the project. Thanks also go Merlin Glodek for his work remastering the tape and in producing the instructional package that follows the match.

Introduction

I watched over a 1,000 games of pro Nine Ball while conducting research for *Play Your Best Nine Ball*. I kept detailed records on 26 matches, from which I created my 500 Game Study of the pros. Some of my discoveries are in *Play Your Best Nine Ball*, and I will be releasing others on the web site and in future publications.

While conducting research of the pro game, I found myself delving into previously uncharted territory, in the process creating a battery of statistics that reveal just how well the great champions play the game. For example, the average pro game lasts only 3.03 innings. Pros make 52.6% of bank shots and 42.7% of their kick shots result in an immediate loss of the game.

Knowing figures like these can give you a true appreciation of the top pros caliber of play. The statistics can also help you to manage your expectations and to provide you with benchmarks for improving your game.

Capelle on 9-Ball started one day when I sat down with a list of shots from a match between Johnny Archer and Efren Reyes. They were the two top ranked players in the world at that time, the double hill game was one of the most thrilling in history, and Accu-Stats commentator Bill Incardona was in verbally in dead stroke. I thought this would be a good choice and one thing lead to another, the result being this companion guide to the match.

I hope you enjoy the match and that you derive many insights into the pro game from the book/video that help you improve your game.

How to Use The Book & Video

Before you start reading my comments, I advise you to watch the match straight through without the book. It is a great match, and I think you will enjoy the drama that leads to an exciting conclusion, as it appeared live.

After you've finished your initial viewing, it is time to get to work on your game. The book is loaded with features that combine with the video to create a valuable learning experience. Work your way through the book/video at your own pace. And don't hesitate to stop the action and refer to the book when something sparks your interest. Make liberal use of special effects, including slow motion.

On any viewing you might wish to emphasize a certain aspect of their games. You might focus on position and pattern play on one viewing, and on the player's stroke and pace of play on the next. While I don't imagine you'll watch the tape 10 times like I did, you will discover something new on every viewing. And these not so little things that you pick up include the fine points that make up a champion.

Throughout Part II and in the Appendix are lists of various types of shots and situations. For example, if you want to study kick shots or pattern play, you'll find a list of these items. Each shot is numbered both in the book and on the tape for easy reference

Part 1 of the book follows the match shot by shot. Listed below are the features and how they appear in Part 1.

Part II is a detailed analysis of the match. In this section you'll discover things about the pro game that have never before appeared in print. After the analysis is a brief summary called **Your Game,** which gives you an important lesson on the subject just covered.

The Format
Players Inning
#1 Archer (example) – This marks the start of a player's inning or turn at the table.
#2 Reyes (example of a second turn or inning.)

The Shots
Break – The results of the break shot.
1-ball, etc. – This denotes a position play or attempted position play.
A, B, or C – One of these letters will appear after 1-ball, 2-ball etc. on position plays. A's are very difficult position routes, B's are moderately challenging routes, and C's are routine position plays.
Safety – Indicates that a safety was played.
Kick – Indicates that a kick shot was played.
BIH – Indicates a player had ball in hand.

The Numbering System
Each shot (excluding the break shot) is numbered. For example, the fifth shot in Game 8 is numbered **8-5.** Each of the numbers corresponds to the number in the upper right corner of the video.

TT 2:48 (example) The total time it took to play a game including racking.

T:12 (example) The time the player took preparing for a key shot. There could be more than one key shot in a game or runout.

ET:7 (example) The time to execute a tough shot. There are 14 shots that took 7 or more seconds.

Learning Experiences

LESSON – These are valuable lessons on position, patterns, strategy and other assorted topics. They are indexed in the appendix.

PATTERN – This is a discussion about a sequence of shots. They are indexed in the appendix.

SloMo – This signals a place where I recommend that you rewind and watch the shot in slow motion, stop action or frame advance. They are indexed in the appendix.

Announcers Discussion – This marks an amusing, informative or educational discussion by either or both announcers. They are indexed in the appendix.

PYBNB – This abbreviation signals a reference to *Play Your Best Nine Ball* where you can find additional information and/or examples of the shot or pattern.

PYBP – This in a reference to *Play Your Best Pool*.

Other Informative Items

Quotes – Cool things from the announcers.

Between Games – Discussions, tips and other interesting information.

The Score – The current score at the end of each game.

The Layout

I rate the difficulty of each layout from the point where a player begins to attempt a runout.

C's are routine runouts, the kind a pro is expected to complete 95-98+% of the time.

B's require at least one particularly difficult shot or position play, or they may contain a series of moderately challenging shots.

A's are very difficult layouts even for pros. They contain an extremely challenging shot and/or several demanding shots.

The Primary Emphasis

Through out the text are 29 selected position plays I feel are particularly instructive. Each shows one or more of the three possible areas for emphasis. The notation for the Primary Emphasis of a successful position play is listed below.

D = Direction is the big key to the shot.

S = Speed is the big key to the shot.

P = Pocketing the ball is the big key to the shot.

When more than one area must be emphasized, the shot naturally goes up in difficulty. When a shot requires more than one area of emphasis, they are ranked in the order of difficulty. For example, on a shot with a **P/S**, the primary emphasis is on pocketing the shot. However, the shot would also require good speed control. A shot rated

S/P/D would require specific attention on all three components, with speed control being most critical.

The Illustrations

The illustrations are drawn perfectly to scale so that you can see exactly how the shots really work at the table. There are no balls that won't fit into the pockets or other techniques that detract from the realism of the shots.

A The cue shows which direction the cue ball is being shot.

B The dashed line shows the path of the cue ball to the object ball, as well as its path after contact.

B-1 The cue ball's path is shown by where the center of the cue ball is traveling. As a result, the line will never touch the rail.

C The dashed circle shows the cue ball's position at contact with the object ball.

D The solid line is the path of the object ball.

E The cue ball with an X inside shows where the cue ball has come to rest. When you see a series of cue balls with an X on one shot, they are illustrating several possible stopping points for the cue ball. On straight in shots when the cue ball stops dead at the point of contact, the X cue ball is used to show both contact and the cue balls ending location.

F You will find descriptive text on the diagrams where appropriate throughout the book.

G It is important to understand the ideal cut angle for a wide variety of shots in Nine Ball. Cut angles are labeled throughout the book on shots where they are critical or instructive.

SAMPLE DIAGRAM

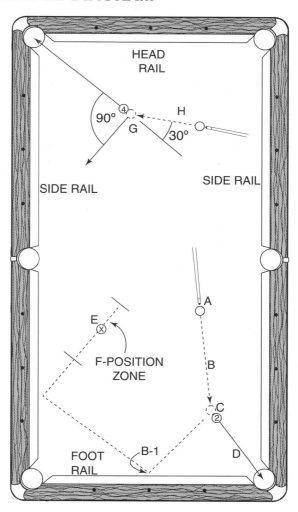

XI

The Spectrum of Speed

There is perhaps no more valuable skill in pool than the ability to consistently stroke the cue ball with the correct speed. When you combine proper speed with expert directional control, you have what it takes to play pinpoint position. Speed control is also vital in playing effective safeties and kick shots.

Nine Ball is played over the entire table, which means you will routinely face a wide variety of position plays, from the softest bunt, to ultra hard draw shots, and all points in between. This means you must become comfortable playing shots all across The Spectrum of Speed, which I developed to quantify speed of stroke.

The softest shots are a rated 1. These shots require an extremely soft stroke. The hardest hit non-break shots are rated 9, or extremely hard. The break is a 10. Break shots are hit anywhere from about 15-30 miles per hour (MPH). Position plays range from a stroke speed of 1.5 MPH for extremely soft shots (1 on the scale) to speeds of 10-12+ MPH for shots that require an extremely hard stroke (9 on the scale). Even though most position plays fall in the 3-7 range, you need be able to play position at either end of the spectrum for your game to be complete.

After every shot you will find a notation showing the speed which the shot was played. This will provide you with some additional insight into the type of stroke used.

The Spectrum of Speed

Speed	MPH	Notation
1 Extremely Soft	1.5	**1ES**
2 Very Soft	2.0	**2VS**
3 Soft	3.0	**3S**
4 Medium Soft	4.0	**4MS**
5 Medium	5.0	**5M**
6 Medium Hard	6.0	**6MH**
7 Hard	7.0	**7H**
8 Very Hard	8.0	**8VH**
9 Extremely Hard	10.0	**9EH**
10 The Break	15+	

Spectrum of Speeds

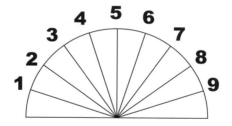

Table of Contents:

PART 2
Capelle on The Pro Game

Shots in Part II of the Video/DVD

Part I – Archer vs. Reyes
The Lag

Archer won the lag. He broke and ran the first game, which proved to be his margin of victory.

Technique Both players used an open bridge. Archer remained frozen until the cue ball hit the near end rail. Reyes likes to lag first. His ball traveled 2.5 diamonds before Archer's began rolling. Archer's cue ball was nearly frozen while Reyes' bounced eight inches off the end cushion.

Game 1 Archer's Strong Start
1 Inn.   TT 2:48

Archer's break and run in the first game sent a statement to Reyes that he was well prepared and had come to play.

LESSON Some players pride themselves on being slow starters who finish strong. You are better off, however, starting fast and keeping the pressure on the whole match, especially if your opponent is easily intimidated by good pool.

#1 Archer Breaks: **Archer** made the 4 and 5-balls.

The Layout: B
The difficult long distance position play on the 1-ball through traffic and the follow shot on the 2-ball are the reasons why this layout is rated B.

Archer

1-1 **1-ball** A 2-rails. Hard draw. **6MH** **T:18**
On this demanding shot Archer had to send the cue ball across table twice and between the 3 and 7-balls. When a pro almost scratches, it is usually a sign the position route was especially difficult, not that they executed the shot poorly. Archer barely overshot the ideal position.
S/D/P Speed is tough because the cue ball is crossing through the position zone. Direction is also a challenge. Archer had to use the correct amount of draw as shown in the diagram.

LESSON Pay close attention to your scratches and near scratches. When you scratch, or almost scratch, do you know the reason why?

1-2 **2-ball** B 1-rail follow. **4MS** **ET:7**
This shot puts Archer in line for what is a fairly routine run out. Archer's route was a two-way position play. He stopped at Position A. If the cue ball had came up short at Position B, he could have played the 3-ball in the upper right corner pocket. Notice Archer's level cue. He is a master at shooting off the rail and over a pocket.

1-3 **3-ball** C 1-rail follow. **2VS**
Archer got a little careless, bumping the 8-ball. The perfect line off the 3-ball would have been 2-3" wide of the 8-ball.

1-4 **6-ball** B 1-rail draw. **6MH**
I would rate this shot a half mistake because the cue

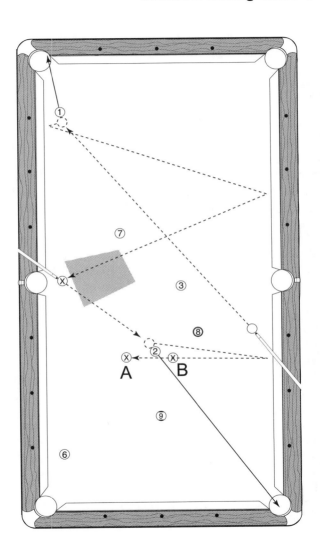

ball stopped several inches short of the ideal spot. Archer now faced a thin cut on the 7-ball.

1-5 **7-ball** B 3-rails follow. **3S**

This shot requires near perfect speed. Great touch! Much tougher than it looks. **PYBNB 105.**

S/P Crossing the position zone is almost never easy.

LESSON Sometimes it is okay to have a slightly thinner cut than the ideal as long as you are not in jeopardy of missing. The thinner angle allows you to play the shot with a softer stroke, which could help to refine your speed control.

1-6 **8-ball** C 0-rail stop. **4MS**

Archer followed the cue ball a few inches with a firm stroke. The shot is stroked like a stop shot **(PYBNB 70)**, only you must cue one eighth tip above center. Firm follow shots allow you to avoid slow rolling shots, thus preventing a roll off.

1-7 **9-ball** 10-degree cut, 2-rails draw. **5M**

How Pros Shoot the 9-Ball

In my 500 Game Study 424 games went the distance. In those 424 games only four 9-balls were missed. This implies the pros play great position, and that they don't miss very often. I'm not going to provide extra commentary on the 9-ball. Nevertheless, I advise you to pay attention to the shots they leave themselves on the 9-ball: they are for the most part relatively short shots with a cut angle under 30-degrees. Notice how they shoot the 9-ball firmly and use the rails to control the cue ball.

Announcers Between Games: There is a discussion on the problems created by the break box, including more fouls. In this match, however, there were no fouls, which indicates how consistently square Archer and Reyes hit the 1-ball.

LESSON Hitting the 1-ball squarely should always be a priority no matter how hard you hit the break shot.

Archer leads 1-0.

Game 2 Easy Run Made Easy
2 Inn.   TT3:00

#1 Archer Breaks: Archer made nothing.

SloMo Look at the sheer power of Archer's break as shown by the follow through. Despite the action of the balls, nothing fell. This is a sign of things to come. If Archer's power break had been working, he probably would have easily won this match.

The Layout: C
This is a very routine runout, the kind pros will complete 95-98% of the time. The big key is getting good position on the 3-ball.

#2 Reyes
2-1   **1-ball** B 2-rails follow. **4MS   T:14   ET:7**

2-2 **2-ball** C 2-rails follow **5M**
Reyes must have really wanted to use the side rail for getting from the 3-ball to the 4-ball as he came close to getting hooked. Instead, he got perfect shape at Position A. The other side of the 3-ball is still very playable even though you can't use the rail for shape on the 4-ball. Playing the route to Position B eliminates the risk of a hook.

S Speed was crucial with the route Reyes used to Position A.

D Direction was the key to playing a more conservative route to Position B.

LESSON When you have a choice between two routes that both will give you good position, choose the one with the least risk if possible.

2-3 **3-ball** C 1-rail draw. **6MH**
2-4 **4-ball** C 0-rail follow. **2VS**
2-5 **5-ball** C 0-rail draw. **4MS**

PATTERN Going to the Rail and Out
Drawing back on the 5-ball gave Reyes an angle on the 6-ball. Now he was able to go to the rail and out to the middle of the table for the 7-ball. This is much easier than playing position for a straight in draw shot on the 6-ball.

LESSON Using the rails and angles correctly greatly simplifies the game.

SloMo Notice how Reyes lets his elbow continue to drop on a draw shot while the cue is forced upwards and out of his bridge by the rail.

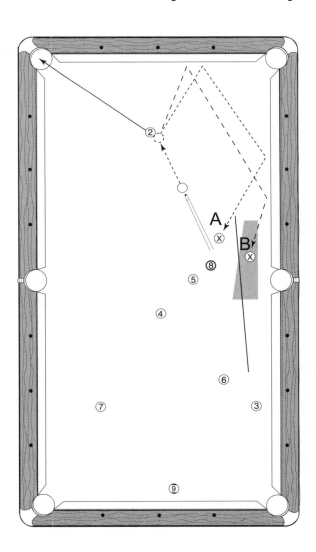

2-6 **6-ball** C 1-rail draw. **5M**
Even though this was a routine position play, it was critical for Reyes to be on the correct side of the 7-ball. See Principle #9, **PYBNB 152**.

2-7 **7-ball** C 1-rail draw **7H**
Once again, Reyes goes to the rail and out to maximize control of the cue ball. Reyes draw shot put him on the right side of the 8-ball.

S It was important for Reyes to use enough speed to get on the right side of the 8-ball. Same principle as in the previous shot.

2-8 **8-ball** C 0-rail draw. **4MS**
Nice touch on a draw floater shot. **PYBNB 74**

2-9 **9-ball** 1-rail 10-degrees follow. **4MS**

LESSON How many times have you failed to run a rack that you think you "should have?" Even though some racks lie easy, it takes skill and concentration to complete the job. One let up and your run could easily end. On easy racks, try to play each shot to perfection. This approach will keep your mind actively involved in the game and it is your best insurance against disaster. In addition, if you play a rack perfectly, that may signal to your opponent that you are a fine player who knows exactly what you're doing. You don't just play pool, you at times play near perfect pool. This could earn a couple of intimidation points. Racks like this are also good for getting in stroke and for developing confidence.

Archer and Reyes are tied 1-1

Game 3 Brush with Disaster
1 Inn.   TT2:30

#1 Reyes Breaks: Reyes makes the 3-ball.

The Layout: C
There are no big problems in this routine layout.
The only "hurdle" to speak of is playing shape on
the combo to start the run.

3-1   **8-ball** (1-8 combo) C 1-rail follow.   **2VS**
SloMo Watch carefully how the 8-ball goes in the
far right side of the pocket. Reyes used the whole
pocket on purpose to control the 1-ball.

LESSON Even though this position shot was not
difficult, it is very easy to miss shape on combos if
you're not extra careful in planning and executing
the shot.

3-2   **1-ball** C 2-rails follow.   **3S   T:11**

SloMo In slow motion you'll see the cue ball brush
the 7-ball in passing! If the cue ball had hit the 7-
ball just a tad fuller, it would have destroyed
Reyes' position on the 2-ball.

LESSON On follow shots in which the cue ball is
going into the rail after contact, the cue ball very
often rebounds at an angle wider than you would
expect it to, you must therefore guard against the
tendency to overshhoot your position zone.

PATTERN   Near Straight in Shape

The cue ball at Position A shows Reyes shape on
the 1-ball. This nearly straight in shot on the 2-
ball allowed him to draw over to Position B for a
perfect angle on the 4-ball. A draw/stun shot using
an eighth of a tip of draw propelled the cue ball to
Position C for the 5-ball. The rest of the runout is
very routine.

Now let's go back to the shot on the 2-ball. If
the cue ball had stopped a few inches on either side
of Position A at Position D or E, getting from the 2-
ball to the 4-ball would have been much tougher.
Position F shows where the cue ball might have
landed if it had struck the 7-ball a little fuller.
Ouch!

3-3   **2-ball** C 0-draw.   **5M**
This shot puts Reyes on the right side of the 4-ball.
3-4   **4-ball** B 0-rail draw.   **6MH**
SloMo Notice how lightly Reyes holds the cue.He
retains his light grip even on his follow through
when 99.8% of all pool players have tightened
their grip considerably.

The remainder of the rack is very routine.
3-5   **5-ball** C 1 rail draw.   **3S**
3-6   **6-ball** C 1 rail draw.   **3S**
3-7   **7-ball** C 0-rail draw.   **5M**
3-8   **9-ball** 0-rail draw.   **3S**

Reyes leads 2-1
Announcers Discussion: The Magician
Incardona discusses Reyes many talents. A Must.

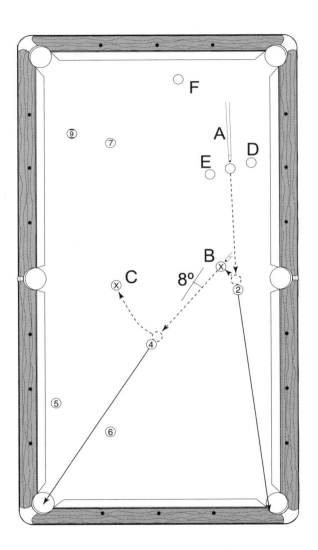

Game 4 Reyes' Massive Draw
5 Inn.   TT5:50

The first three games were relatively tame, routine runouts. The rest of the match features a roller coaster ride encompassing most all aspects of the game.

#1 Reyes Breaks: Reyes made nothing.

#2 Archer
4-1   **1-ball** B 1-rail follow. **4MS**
Archer faced a layout that has a huge problem with congestion (the 4, 5, 7, and 9-balls). He came up well short of side pocket shape and was forced to play a safety.
S/P Speed was the critical item on this testy shot and Archer unfortunately fell short of the mark.
4-2   **Safety 3S**   Archer played a soft follow shot safe and left a window for Reyes.

LESSON Archer did not walk over to the left side of the table to see if there was a window between the cluster. If he had, perhaps he would have played the safety with more precision. Don't forget to survey the table from more than one angle!

"When this man concentrates he's unstoppable if given an opportunity." **Incardona** on Reyes

#3 Reyes
4-3   **2-ball** C 1-rail follow.   **3S**

SloMo This shot offers a good view of one of Reyes bridging techniques on the rail.

4-4 **3-ball** Misses thin cut. **2VS ET:8**

> **LESSON** This is a two way shot. If Reyes makes the 3-ball, he runs out. If he misses, it's a safety. Reyes accomplished two big objectives on this shot: he broke a cluster and he hooked Archer.

Technique Reyes' backstroke on this finesse cut shot was only half as long as his gargantuan bridge. If Archer had played this shot, his bridge would have been on the cloth.

#4 Archer
4-5 **Kicked** 1 rail and missed. **9EH**
Archer tried to cut the 3-ball on the left side so the cue ball would travel down for the 4-ball. The idea was solid, but he failed to allow for the sharp rebound angle created by the hard stroke as the announcers mentioned. This was Archer's only foul in the entire match. See **PYBNB 334-335.**

The Layout: B
This layout is tougher than it appears. The position plays are not very difficult, but each one needs to be executed just right. The 6, 7, and 8-balls are all near the same rail, which adds to the challenge as we'll see in a moment.

#5 Reyes BIH
Viewing Tip: Always pay special attention to where the pros place the cue ball with ball-in-hand, and to their resulting position. In this case,

Reyes placed the cue ball about a foot from the 3-ball, setting up a straight back draw shot.

4-6 **3-ball** B 1-rail draw. **6MH   T1: 22**
SloMo Stop the action and you'll see Reyes' tip on or just above the cloth at address. When he strikes the cue ball, the tip is much higher. Observe Reyes' extended follow through. Also notice how smoothly yet quickly he removes himself from the table to avoid the cue ball.

4-7 **4-ball** C 1-rail draw.   **5M**
Reyes played the 4-ball with perfect speed, which set up the ideal angle from the 5-ball to the 6-ball. It is this kind of simple looking stuff that enables the pros to make the game look so easy.
S/D An eighth of a tip of draw with superb touch.

4-8 **5-ball** C 1-rail draw.   **4MS**
4-9 **6-ball** C 1-rail draw.   **5M**
Reyes failed to come far enough off the rail and ended up on the wrong side of the 7-ball.

PATTERN The Dominos Are Falling

The diagram shows the shots that led up to the 7-ball. Reyes left himself a shallow angle (15-degrees) at Position A for the 6-ball. This led to shape on the wrong side of the 7-ball at Position B. If Reyes had obtained a slightly larger angle on the 6-ball at Position C, he could have easily sent the cue ball to Position D for the 7-ball. From D, he could have then played the easy route to Position E for the 8-ball. However, I'm glad he missed shape or else we would not have been treated to his spectacular shot on the 7-ball.

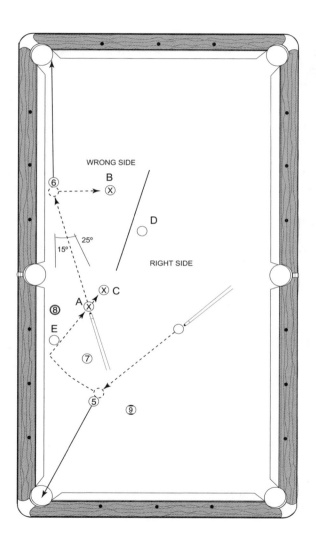

LESSON The Domino Theory: Be careful to avoid that one big mistake that can put you out of line to where it is impossible to recover position without playing an extraordinary shot. The 5-ball was domino #1 while the 6-ball was domino #2, both of which led up to Reyes' shot on the 7-ball.

4-10 **7-ball** A 3-rails draw. **9EH T:17 ET:8 P/S** The direction takes care of itself as there is plenty of room for position on the 8-ball. Hitting the shot accurately with a very hard stroke is the major challenge.

SloMo This is an extremely strong recovery shot from the wrong side of the 7-ball. Notice how well Reyes stays down on the shot. His tip is well above the cloth at the conclusion of his follow through, which is an indication of the magnitude of his elbow drop on a power draw shot. Pay special attention to the cue ball as it curves dramatically when crossing the table after contact. Shown in **PYBNB 107**

LESSON Reyes used six warm up strokes while getting set to play this shot. Most good players add at least 1-4 warm up strokes to their routine when faced with a difficult shot.

"That looked like a Mike Massey draw shot as well as he hit that." **David Maddux**

4-11 **8-ball** C 1-rail follow. **2VS**
4-12 **9-ball** 0-rail 5-degrees. **3S**

Reyes leads 3-1

Game 5 Working a Mistake
8 Inn.   TT8:50

#1 Reyes Breaks: Reyes made the 1-ball on the break. This softer break, with the 1-ball going into the side rail, was a forerunner to the soft break used today under certain conditions.

Layout: A The 1-ball is the big key.

5-1 **2-ball** A 1-rail. **8VH**
Reyes elevated his cue slightly to add speed to the cue ball, causing it to rebound more to the right off the end rail. This made it hard to control the speed of the shot, and resulted in a hook.

LESSON This error occurs quite often on 1-rail routes from one end of the table to the other, which are tough to execute with precision.

5-2 **Safety** Reyes played a soft half masse and hit the 3-ball. Notice the 45-degree cue elevation for this touchy shot.

#2 Archer
5-3 **Safety 1ES** (left handed)
Archer began to work on Reyes position play error by playing a safety on the 3-ball, hooking Reyes.
Announcers Discussion: Listen to the announcers discussion of strategy.

LESSON When your opponent makes a mistake, you must work it to your fullest advantage. Archer kept Reyes on the run for seven innings until he was able to cash in on Reyes' initial mistake.

#3 Reyes
5-4 Intentional Foul
Reyes played an intentional foul, shooting the 4-ball down table to make a run out more difficult.

LESSON This is a very effective strategy against players whose position play is not particularly sharp. However, it often only forestalls an inevitable loss of game among fine players. Most of the time, but not always.

Announcers: Incardona discussed how separating the balls is a good strategy when playing an intentional foul.

#4 Archer BIH
5-5 3-ball C 1-rail draw. 2VS
Announcers: Archer took his time planning the shot. He did not follow the announcer's strategy.

5-6 Safety 3S Archer played safe and hooked
Reyes. See **PYBNB 292**.

Announcer: Incardona raised the question of whether Archer hit the 5-ball with his cue or the cue ball. The replay shows it was his cue.

#5 Reyes
5-7 Kick 2VS
Reyes played a soft rail first hit, leaving Archer with an easy safety. He should have taken a more aggressive shot. He could have tried to hit the ball hard and hope for a roll. Now it is very seldom that you can second-guess Reyes' choice on kick shots,

but this is one glaring exception.

LESSON Sometimes the blast-and-hope shot is preferable to strategic kicking with speed control. Sometimes, as in this case, but not usually.

#6 Archer
5-8 Safety 3S
He played a classic 2-rail safety route, hooking Reyes. **PYBNB 281**.

#7 Reyes
5-9 7H Kick
Reyes kicked 1-rail, hits and scratched.
Reyes made excellent contact with the 4-ball, and was a bit unlucky to scratch as the cue ball barely toppled into the side pocket. If the cue ball had stopped short of the side, Archer would have had a difficult shot or safety.

LESSON Kicking is far from a precise science, even for the world's best kicker. Give all kick shots your best effort, and be glad when they work out. But don't be too bummed when they don't.

The Layout: C
There are no problems in this extremely routine runout. The key shot is position on the 6-ball.

#8 Archer BIH
5-10 4-ball C 1-rail draw. **3S**   **T:13**

PATTERN **Down the Line is a Winner**
Archer kept the cue ball a diamond from the left
side rail to set up the key position play from the 5
to the 6-ball. Archer then used a 2-rail route to
play down the line position on the 6-ball. (See
Principle #12, **PYBNB 158.**) Archer's path was at
a slight angle to the 6-ball. If he had drawn the cue
ball a little more and/or hit the 5-ball a little fuller,
it's path would have been more in line with the 6-
ball as shown. A stop shot on the 6-ball would have
then yielded ideal position on the 7-ball. While I'm
nit picking here, the idea is to show how you can
refine your position play on even the most routine
shots.

5-11 **5-ball** C 2-rails outside draw. **3S**
S/D Speed was critical on Archer's path.

5-12 **6-ball** C 0-rail draw. **5M**
5-13 **7-ball** C 0-rail draw. **6MH**
5-14 **8-ball** C 2-rails follow. **5M**
5-15 **9-ball** 5-degrees 1-rail draw. **5M**

LESSON Don't throw in the towel when you're in
a tough spot and a loss looks likely. Make your
opponent earn everything. You just might be able
to turn the tables with some heads up maneuver.

Archer held the upper hand after Reyes' initial
mistake, nevertheless:
"He still had to work hard to earn this game."
Incardona

Reyes leads 3-2

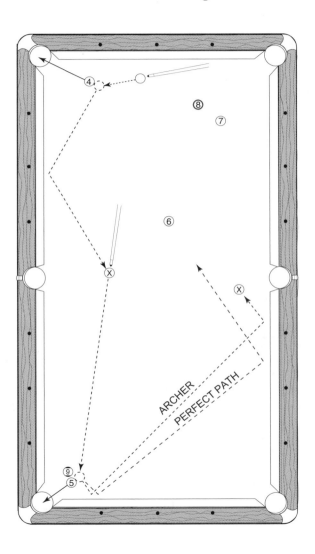

Game 6 Reyes Splits Uprights
2 Inn.   TT3:24

#1 Archer Breaks: **Archer** made nothing.
Discussion: Incardona discusses the break.

The Layout: B+
The first shot is often the big key to running out.
Reyes must play several moderately difficult position plays to run this rack, including the group of
three balls near the top rail.

#2 Reyes
6-1 **1-ball** A 1-rail draw through traffic. **6MH**
Reyes played pinpoint shape through traffic. This
shot was risky, but if Reyes had run into either the
3 or 6-ball, he still would probably have had a shot,
or at worst a safety.
D/S Avoiding a hook with directional control was
tough. Reyes also needed to get past the blockers.
6-2 **2-ball** C 0-rail draw. **4MS**
Reyes hit another ball to kill the cue ball's speed
for position. See other examples, **PYBNB 124-125**.
6-3 **3-ball** B 1-rail draw. **6MH**
There is a tendency to use excessive draw on this
position play. Reyes wound up at Position A. The
preferable spot for the 4-ball is anywhere in the
position zone, such as at Position B.
S Speed was crucial on the route Reyes took.
D Direction is the key element to reaching the
position zone.

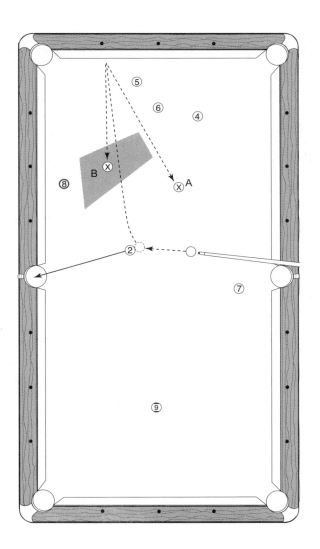

LESSON When the object ball is past the side pocket and the cue ball is going directly to the end rail and out, you are facing a very tricky position play. It is very hard to make the cue ball bounce off the end rail at a 90-degree angle to the rail.

6-4 **4-ball** B 2-rails draw/outside. **4MS** **T:20**
This is a finesse shot that requires precise draw control (cueing) to avoid hitting the 6-ball.
6-5 **5-ball** C 1-rail follow. **3S**

SloMo Technique This shot gives an excellent side view of Reyes' grip hand. In slow motion you can see it actually moves back and forth along his cue! Use the ring on his cue as a point of reference.

6-6 **6-ball** B 2-rails draw outside. **5M**
A slightly shallower cut angle on the 7-ball would have been even better.
S Reyes needed to get to or past the 7-ball.

6-7 **7-ball** C 1-rail follow. **3S**
D/S Good directional control leads to Position B. Speed is also critical.

PATTERN **Half Mistake Loses Angle**
Reyes commits a half mistake, leaving himself a shallow angle on the 8-ball at Position A. Even though he got out, he was forced to use a hard draw stroke on the 8-ball. In the long run his percentages would be better if he played to Position B. With the larger cut angle, Reyes could have easily sent the cue ball across and down table to Position C for the 9-ball.

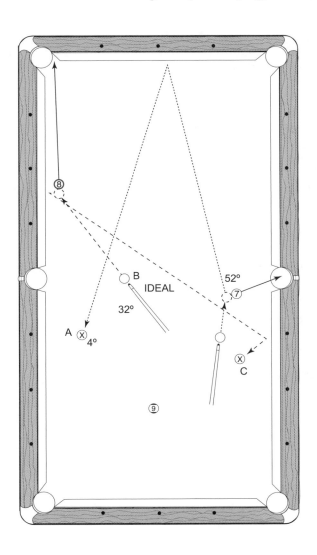

LESSON The most direct route between two points is a straight line (as Reyes played the 8-ball). Nevertheless, in pool the best way may be the longer route as shown.

6-8 **8-ball** B 1 rail draw. **7H**
6-9 **9-ball** 30-degrees 3-rails draw. **6MH**
Reyes played a classic 3-rail route on the 9-ball, sending the cue ball to the right side rail, midway between the side and corner pockets.

LESSON Shooting the 9-ball with a firm stroke can alleviate the effect of nerves. And be sure to "play position" away from the pockets by routing the cue ball with care.

LESSON This was not a perfect runout, but it demonstrates how a pro gets out by playing acceptable shape at times, and then recovering to excellent position on the subsequent shot.

Reyes leads 4-2

Game 7 9-Ball on the Snap
#1 1 Inn. TT:42

#1 Reyes Breaks: Reyes made the 9-ball and the 3-ball.
The 9-ball was kissed in. Does that make it a luckier shot than if it went in directly? I would say no,

because a 9-ball on the break is mostly luck anyway. What's your view?

Reyes leads 5-2

Game 8   Miscue City
4 Inn. TT2:57
#1 Reyes Breaks: Reyes made the 4-ball and 7-ball.

SloMo Technique This gives you a great look at Reyes' break. The cue ball took five frames to travel 48.8" into the 1-ball (30 frames per second) or about a sixth of a second. This translates into roughly 17MPH. If you figure a possible half frame error on either side, the maximum speed Reyes hit the cue ball was 21MPH.

8-1 Safety 2VS
Reyes played a safety and left a hit.

Announcers Discussion The announcers discuss the wisdom of copying your opponents break position and speed if your break isn't working and theirs is.

#2 Archer
8-2 Safety 6MH
Archer played safe, leaving Reyes a long cut. This is an example of using distance as a strategic weapon when a hook is not likely or even possible.

LESSON When playing safe, distance is a good defense when a hook is not likely, and position is unlikely even if your opponent makes the shot.

#3 Reyes
8-3 **1-ball** A 2-rails follow.   **H7   ET:7**
P/D/S Good direction avoids a hook behind the 3 and 9-ball. Good speed control avoids a thin cut on the 2-ball.
Reyes used six warm up stokes to prepare for this table length 75-degree cut. He got shape on the 2-ball but he unfortunately tied up the 3 and 9-balls. The cue ball traveled 23.5 feet on three trips across the table and was a scant two inches wide of perfection! A tough pill for anyone to swallow. See **PYBNB 327.**

8-4 **2-ball - Miscues**
Reyes committed a rare mistake for a pro when he miscued, knocking the cue ball off the table.

#4 Archer **BIH**
8-5 **2-ball** C 1 rail follow.   **2VS**
8-6 3-9 <u>combo</u>, easy.

"Archer has a sledgehammer break but it is not paying off for him." **Incardona**

Reyes leads 5-3

Game 9 The Rain Dance
3 Inn.   TT4:25
While the balls were taking their places, Archer tried to urge the 9-ball into the pocket with his "rain dance," according to Maddux. This provided a little comic relief in a very intense struggle.

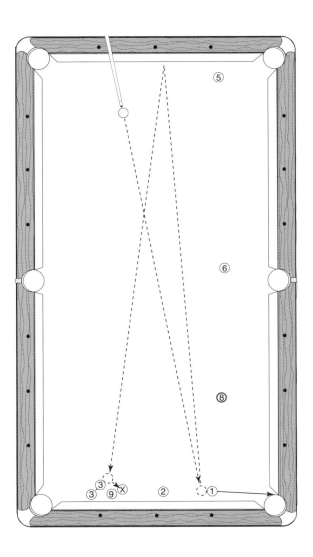

#1 Archer Breaks: Archer made nothing, leaving the 9-ball in the jaws.

#2 Reyes
9-1 **Push Out 2VS**
Reyes pushed out and Archer wisely passed.

9-2 **Safety – 4MS** Reyes safety left Archer with a long shot.
See **PYBNB 312 and 271.**
Analysis: After Archer came up empty on the break, Reyes was in a predicament. He failed to combo in the 9-ball, as Incardona noted, opening the doors for a short rack victory. Reyes was a little unlucky with his safety. It could have easily resulted in a hook behind the 5-ball. He wound up leaving Archer a long tough shot on the 1-ball and a possible billiard on the 9-ball.

LESSON In the position Reyes faced after the break, most amateurs would be wise to sink the 9-ball on the push out, even if that means their opponent ultimately winds up with ball-in-hand.

#3 Archer
9-3 **1 & 9-ball Billiard. 9EH T:38 ET:9**
Archer pocketed the 1-ball and then the 9-ball on a billiard. See page **PYBNB 24**. Archer wisely surveyed the table before shooting this shot.

SloMo The diagram and tape show that the cue ball took off at a 90-degree angle to the 1-ball's line to the pocket directly towards perfect contact with the 9- ball. This line of travel was a result of

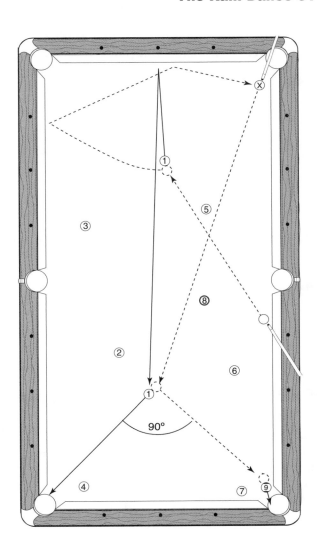

perfect cueing and speed by Archer.

Notice how well Archer stayed with the shot until the cue ball was far down the table. On the 10 scale I rated this shot a 9.8 because: 1) he had to bridge over the pocket, 2) he had about a quarter inch clearance past the 5-ball, and 3) it's a long shot across the diagonal of the table.

LESSON Archer beared down on this shot as evidenced by his eight warm up strokes compared to his average of 3.36. When you are faced with a tough shot, take a little more time setting up and add some warm up strokes to your routine.

"You cannot hit a ball any better than he just did."
Incardona

Announcers Between Games: *"Usually you'll try something twice but no more than twice.* **Incardona** on switching break position if balls aren't falling.

Reyes leads 5-4

Game 10 Second Chance Victory
4 Inn. TT5:17

#1 Archer Breaks: Archer made nothing.
The balls scattered beautifully on this extremely well struck break, but nothing fell. Breaks like this are the bane of all players as there is not much worse than coming up empty and leaving your opponent an easy run out.

SloMo At one point on Archers extremely long follow through you'll see that the cue ball looks like it is stuck to the tip of his cue after it has blasted into the 1-ball.

Layout: C+
The 3-ball is the only major hurdle. When multiple balls are in the middle portion of the table, they severely cut down on the position lanes. So even though the balls are widely scattered, this rack is not mere target practice.

#2 Reyes
10-1 **1-ball** C 1-rail follow. **4MS**
10-2 **2-ball** B 2-rails follow. **4MS T:41**

LESSON Reyes took a long time planning the shot on the 2-ball which, to most players, might have looked like a routine shot. When you see a player of this caliber take lots of time studying the layout, it is always for a very good reason. What looks to be routine is often far from it.

10-3 **3-ball** A 0-rail draw. **8VH**
This long straight back draw shot takes excellent technique.

SloMo This shot showcased Reyes' approach to a long draw shot. Use slow motion and freeze frame. Observe how low and level Reyes' cue is through contact. Notice how he stays down on the shot, as well as his long and relaxed follow through.

10-4 **4-ball** C 2-rails draw/outside. **6MH**

Reyes came up a little short of ideal position on the 5-ball at Position A. Pros routinely recover from this kind of half mistake, but not this time. From long range at Position A, Reyes was forced to float the cue ball sideways into the gap between the 7 and 8-balls for position on the 5-ball. The result was a hook.

If Reyes had used a little less draw on the 4-ball, the cue ball would have stopped near Position B. From Position B it would have been much easier to send the cue ball into the position zone.

10-5 **5-ball** C 0-rail draw. **4MS**

Reyes hooked himself.

D The direction was controlled primarily with cueing. Reyes hit just a hair too much draw.

LESSON Reyes sets up with his cue very low. During his final stroke he adjusts to hit higher on the cue ball. This technique causes him to occasionally put excessive draw on the cue ball. If you have a preference for hitting high or low on the cue ball, make sure it doesn't lead to position errors on certain shots.

10-6 **Kick Shot 9EH**

Reyes kicked 1 rail and hit, but left Archer with a safety opportunity. Reyes is a master at using the correct speed on kick shots. So when you see him blast a kick like this you can be pretty sure it is the correct strategy. The blast shot was preferable because it was late in the game, there were few potential blockers, and the balls were widely

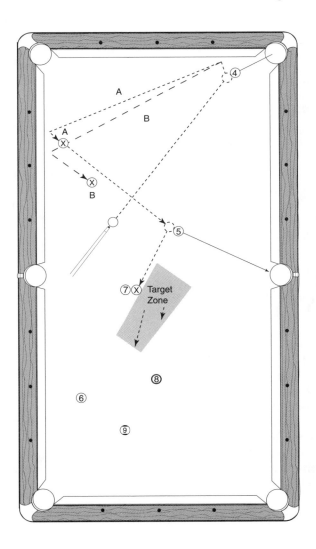

spread, which negates the chances of playing a soft kick/hook safety.

"It's not often that you're going to see Reyes make an unforced error." **Incardona**

#3 Archer
10-7 Safety 3S
He played safe, but failed to hook Reyes.

LESSON Once again, the ability to send the cue ball off a cushion or two and snooker your opponent is a vital weapon that should be added to your defensive arsenal. In this case, Archer will lose the game because of this mistake.

Layout: B
This four-ball run rates a "B" because the bank is probably a 70% shot. The remaining three balls are target practice.

#4 Reyes
10-8 6-ball A 3-rails follow on bank. 8VH T:7
Diagrammed in **PYBNB 116.**
Reyes' choice of playing safe or going for the bank was strictly a judgment call. If he was not sure of the rails, he might have played safe instead. Reyes took only seven seconds in the preparation phase of the shot cycle. This indicated there was no doubt he was going for the bank and that he gave little consideration to playing safe.

Announcers Discussion Maddux mentioned that Reyes may have gone for the bank because he was disgusted with his shot on the 5-ball.

LESSON **Mental Game** A poor shot can serve as a wake up call. It can get your adrenaline going and prepare you for a strong showing. On the other hand, you can't let one mistake upset you to the point where you commit additional errors. For many players, the correct response to a shot like Reyes' on the 5-ball would be to remain calm, play a safety on the 6-ball, and stick to your game plan of playing the percentages.

LESSON Amateurs in this position often are better off playing safe, especially if their opponent is poor at kicking.

10-9	**7-ball**	C 1-rail follow.	**3S**
10-10	**8-ball**	C 1 rail draw.	**5M**
10-11	**9-ball**	5-degree 0-rail draw.	**5M**

Announcers Between Games: Maddux talks about the positives of playing on camel colored cloth. Sorry, but I'm a green cloth purist and trust you are too.

Reyes leads 6-4

"Archer in his chair is really having a hard time dealing with this because he's usually the player who gets paid off on the break." **Incardona**

LESSON When your break isn't working, there are still many other ways you can win a match, as Archer proves throughout this contest. This is even more true at the amateur level of play.

Game 11 Collision Course
2 Inn.   TT3:51

#1 Reyes Breaks: Reyes made the 5 and 7-balls.

The Layout: B The main hurdle is getting good position on the 2 and 3-balls. This is the kind of layout a pro expects to run. When they fail to run out and lose a game like this and the match, they always look back and say "I should have run that rack, and if I did, the score would have been..."

11-1   1-ball B+ 1-rail draw. 6MH

S/P If the 1-ball had been struck a little harder, Reyes could have avoided contact on the following shot. But this kind of speed control is difficult on a shot like the 1-ball. See **PYBNB 84.**

11-2   2-ball B 1-rail draw. 6MH

It is nearly impossible for Reyes to avoid the 3-ball because the cue ball's path down the stun line points at the left edge of the 3-ball. In addition, Reyes will lose control of the cue ball if he doesn't use draw. If he used a bit more draw, he would have knocked the 3-ball a little further from the rail and perhaps given himself a better angle for getting position on the 4-ball.

LESSON If you can't avoid hitting a ball, make sure you plan for something good to happen after contact.

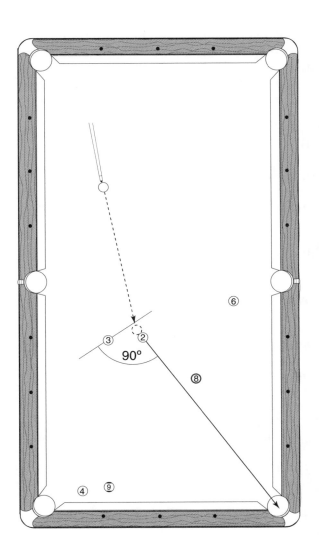

11-3 **3-ball** B 1-rail draw, no position.**7H T:31**
Reyes tried to regain position by playing close to
the 4-ball.but failed. If he used less speed or draw,
the cue ball would have struck the 9-ball fuller,
resulting in a shot on the 4-ball. Regulating speed
and draw on a shot like this is not easy.

"Whenever Reyes goes to his head, he's in trouble."
Bill Incardona:

LESSON Running into balls is a leading cause of
loss of position. The error results from poor planning and/or poor execution.

11-4 **Safety**
Reyes' safety left Archer a shot.

The Layout: C+
This layout rates a C+ only because the 4-ball is a
tricky shot. The rest is routine.

#2 Archer
11-5 **4-ball** B 0-rail draw. **4MS   T:16**
11-6 **6-ball** B 1 rail draw. **4MS**
11-7 **8-ball** C 1 rail draw. **5M**

LESSON Archer played the shot off the side rail
using a firm draw stroke. This was better than
slow rolling the 7-ball into the corner with follow.
This fine point of position play is one of those little
things that raises your runout percentages.

11-8 **9-ball** 5-degrees 1-rail follow. **3S**

Reyes leads 6-5

Game 12 Double Kiss of Death
1 Inn.   TT1:07

This shot evens up the 9-balls on the break at one each, demonstrating that the pool gods are sometimes fair in the short run, which is not normally the case in a single set. In my 500 Game Study, 11 9-balls were pocketed on the break. Two of the 11 were made in this match in the space of six games!!

#1 Archer Breaks: Archer made the 9-ball and the 8-ball. The 9-ball got kissed twice on its way to its destination in a corner pocket. Once again, I ask you: was this luckier than making the 9-ball straight in on the break?
Note: Archer can be seen cleaning the cue ball, as he does frequently before breaking.

Announcers Between Games Maddux commented that Archer took some speed off his break, used Reyes break position, and made two balls.

LESSON Copying your opponent's break position and speed is a smart tactic when their break is working and yours isn't. So always pay attention to your and your opponents results on the break.

Score tied 6-6

Archer does a rack inspection.

Game 13 Roadmap Runout
2 Inn. TT2:46
#1 Archer Breaks: Archer made nothing.

The Layout: C+
The 3 and 4-balls are the key shots.

#2 Reyes
13-1 **1-ball** C 1-rail follow. **2VS**
13-2 **2-ball** C 0-rail draw. **2VS**

PATTERN The Right Side to Avoid a Collision
If the cue ball had traveled 2-3" short of Position A, the 8-ball would have come into play on the 3-ball. If Reyes had played to the other side of the 3-ball to Position B, he would have eliminated the chances of running into the 8-ball. He would have also avoided the stretch shot on the 3-ball.

13-3 **3-ball** B 2-rail inside follow. **6MH**

SloMo This recovery shot showcased Reyes' long and straight follow through. The cue ball hopped over an inch off the table after contacting the 3-ball before it took off running. See **PYBNB 93.**

13-4 **4-ball** B 2-rail draw. **4MS** **T:12**
Reyes went deep into the corners to avoid the 9-ball. This shot is the key to the run out. For more on this see **PYBNB 65.** The cue ball closely followed a straight in line to position on the 5-ball.
D Direction was the critical component on this down the line position play.

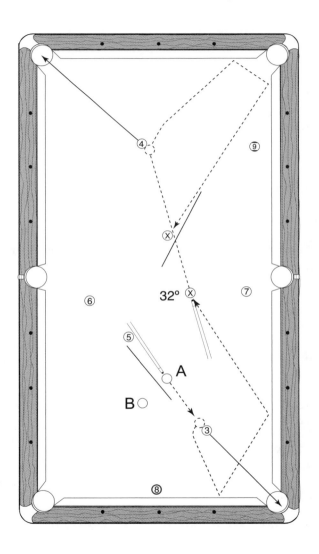

LESSON The pros can come very close to a pocket on purpose without scratching, which shows their exquisite cue ball control. How close can you come to the pocket without scratching? For another example see **PYBNB 95.**

13-5 **5-ball** C 0-rail draw. **4MS**
13-6 **6-ball** C 1-rail follow. **3S**
Reyes has a preference for bridging on the rails, even if it means using a 20" long bridge as in this example. There must be some advantage that he gains from this, but I haven't a clue. If you have tried this with success, please contact me and let me know why it works so well for you.

Announcers Discussion Incardona talks about how Reyes is unhappy with his game, but that he will probably get it going soon enough.

LESSON Mental Game You've got to hang tough and give each shot your very best. Learn how to win without your "A" game. At the same time, retain the thought that your best game could return at any moment. After all, it could!

13-7 **7-ball** C 1-rail draw. **4MS**
13-8 **8-ball** C 2-rails inside follow. **5M**
A good basic 2-rail route using inside english. **PYBNB 91.**
13-9 **9-ball** 10-degrees 1-rail draw. **6MH**

SloMo This is a good rear view of Reyes' stroke. Slow down the action and use frame advance and you will see how his wrist cocks slightly at the end of his backstroke. This shows how relaxed Reyes' arm and wrist are during the transition. The transition is the most crucial part of the stroke and is a place where far too many players tense up in anticipation of the hit.

Reyes leads 7-6

Game 14 Heads I Win, Tails You Lose 3 Inn. TT3:37

#1 Reyes Breaks: Reyes made the 1 and 6-balls. This break offers a good full table view.

14-1 Two Way Safety 5M

Reyes used superb sideways draw control on this two-way shot on the 2-ball. If he made the bank, he would have been in position for the 3-ball. But since he missed, Archer ended up in big trouble.

#2 Archer
14-2 Kick Shot 6MH

He kicked 1-rail and left Reyes a shot. The odds of Archer pocketing the 2-ball were quite slim. If Archer had used a very hard stroke and played for a roll, he would have given himself a much better chance for something good to happen.

LESSON When you are kicking a long distance to the open end of the table and the chances of making the ball are slim, your best bet may be to shoot firmly and try to separate the balls, possibly even resulting in a hook.
See **PYBNB 354.**

The Layout B+

The first shot is often the big key to running out in the pro game. Still, Reyes had to negotiate a ball in the middle of the table (the 4-ball), which can't be taken for granted.

#3 Reyes

14-3 **2-ball** A 3-rails outside draw. **6MH T:24**
Reyes deftly executed a 3-rail route through traffic on the first ball. Often the key to running out is "getting in line" for the next ball.

Announcers: Incardona on why a lesser player won't get position: *"They wouldn't understand the speed of the shot as well as he (Reyes) does."*

SloMo This offers a good view of how Reyes sets up with the cue low, but hits it near center!

LESSON It may not always be a good idea to imitate the technique(s) of your favorite players.

14-4 **3-ball** C 1-rail follow. **5M**
D Good directional control gave Reyes several options for playing the 4-ball. His choice depended on the speed of the shot on the 3-ball.

PATTERN Setting Up the Correct Angle

Reyes used the 3-ball to set up a relatively shallow angle on the 4-ball, which enabled him to go to the rail and out for the 5-ball. When shaping balls in the middle of the table, a cut angle of 15-20 degrees is ideal for to sending the cue ball to a rail and out.

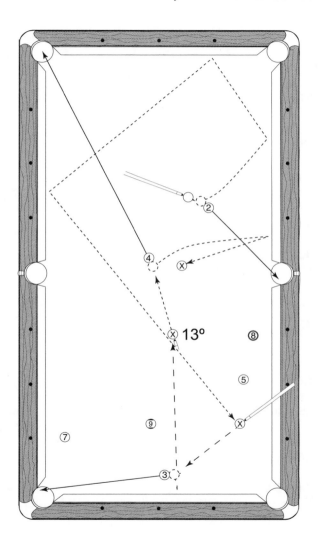

Straight in shape on the 4-ball would have been near perfect. In most cases, however, it is generally too difficult to play shape for a straight in shot.

14-5 **4-ball** B 1-rail draw. **6MH**
This well-executed draw/stun shot was hit with a very firm stroke.
14-6 **5-ball** C 1-rail draw. **6MH**
The rest of the rack is very routine.

Announcers Discussion: Incardona gives a discourse on pro position.
#1 *"So often you find yourself coming up one or one and a half feet short because you're fearful of scratching or going behind another ball."*
#2 *"But when you have the ability and the touch and the finesse and the confidence like the players we're watching right now, I mean that's how the game is supposed to be played and that's why all these people are here in attendance. Because they've come to see the greatest players in the world."*

14-7 **7-ball** B 2-rails follow. **3S**
Reyes correctly played to the short side for shape on the 8-ball in the far corner pocket. Reyes' decision to violate Principle #10 (Play to the long side when possible and practical) demonstrates that pool is full of exceptions to the rules. See **PYBNB 154-156** and **PYNBN 172**.

LESSON On shots like the 7-ball, it is much easier to play position by going into the rail and out as Reyes did, rather than trying to make the cue ball stop short of the rail.

14-8 **8-ball** C 1-rail draw. **3S**
14-9 **9-ball** 5-degrees draw. **6MH**

Reyes leads 8-6.

Game 15 BIH = Run Out
2 Inn. TT2:47
#1 Reyes Breaks: Reyes made the 1-ball directly into the side pocket using a soft break.

The Layout: A
It is an A at this point because the 2-ball is such a difficult shot.

Reyes Misses
15-1 **2-ball** Reyes missed and scratched. **9EH D/S** Even though Reyes missed, check out his route to the 3-ball: it is a 4-rail around the table route that required an extremely hard stroke.

LESSON When pros miss, it is not by much due to their accuracy. When you miss, pay attention to the side of the miss (under cut or over cut) and to the magnitude of the error. By doing so, you can begin to reprogram your mind for the correct impression of that shot when it comes up again.

LESSON Reyes would not have scratched if he had made the shot, as Incardona noted. When you miss a ball, you can't assume the cue ball would have ended up in the exact same location.

"(Reyes) Scratching in the corner was a delight for Archer." **Incardona**

Layout: C+
The key is the 4, 5 and 6-ball sequence. Position on the 6-ball makes the rest of the rack very easy.

#2 Archer BIH
15-2 **2-ball** C 0-rail follow.   **3S T:14**
Archer placed the cue ball about eight inches from the 2-ball which is the ideal distance in most cases. You don't want to place the cue ball so close that you have to stretch for the shot.
15-3 **3-ball** C 0-rail draw.   **4MS**
Archer most likely played to this side of the 3-ball so he could avoid stretching.
15-4 **4-ball** C 1-rail outside draw.   **4MS**
Archer set up a perfect angle on the 5-ball.

Announcers Discussion Incardona on how the champions recognize the key ball.

15-5 **5-ball** B 1-rail follow.   **4MS**

PATTERN   Simple But Effective
This very well played 1-rail route is nothing fancy. It's just the kind of perfect execution that enables the pros to make the game look so darn easy. Archer, by the way, is a leading exponent of 1-rail position. The 5-ball put Archer in ideal position to go from the 6 to the 7-ball.

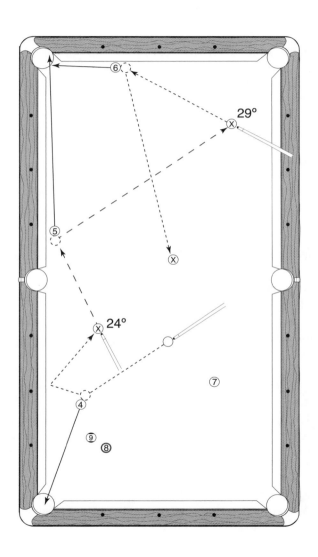

15-6 **6-ball** C 1 rail stun. **5M**
D This down the line position play makes the game look easier than it really is.

"Now all Archer needs to be concerned with is staying focused." **Incardona**

15-7 **7-ball** C 0-rail draw. **4MS**
15-8 **8-ball** C 0-rail draw. **5M**
15-9 **9-ball** 0-rail stop. **4MS**

Between Games: *"The stubborn Archer isn't about to let Reyes run away with the match."* **Incardona**

Reyes leads 8-7.

Game 16 A Magician at Work
4 Inn. TT5:14

#1 Archer Breaks: Archer made nothing. Watch the 5-ball spinning near the pocket.

The Layout: A
Announcers Discussion
Incardona talks about the problem 4-ball on the left side rail. When a ball is frozen to the rail near the side pocket you've almost always got a major problem. **PYNBN 251.**

LESSON If there is some way to move a ball that's frozen to the rail near the side pocket like the 4-ball, do it.

#2 Reyes
16-1 **5-ball** C 0-rail follow on 1-5 combo.
3S **T:23**
16-2 **1-ball** C 1-rail draw. **4MS T:20**
Reyes overshot his position zone on this demanding position play. This shot demonstrated the dangers of crossing through a zone, which requires near perfect speed control. See Principle #12, **PYBNB 158.**

If Reyes was playing shape for the 2-9 combo because of the 4-ball, as Incardona mentioned, he attempted to land in a minute shape zone.

16-3 Safety **2VS**
Reyes played safe off the 2-ball and left Archer a long shot.

#3 Archer
16-4 He missed a long shot. **6MH T:20 ET:7**
SloMo Once again, when the pros miss, they miss real close. You'll see Archer's head start to move a split second before his tip contacts the cue ball.

LESSON Even though Archer missed, he was justified in taking the shot because of his ability as a shotmaker. In addition, at higher levels of competition where there are fewer opportunities to shoot, players dislike giving up the table. They often would rather go down shooting than engage in a safety/kick war with a crafty opponent, especially one like Reyes who is a master of defense.

> **LESSON**: The diagram shows a safety that takes advantage of the wall of blockers. (The 3, 6, and 8-balls). See **PYBNB 302**. If safeties are your strength and shotmaking is not, the safety is the better choice. The Lesson: there is not always one best shot for all players, but there is usually one best shot for your game.

The Layout: A
The problem 4-ball is still on the rail. In addition, it will be tough to get from the 6-ball in the middle of the table to the 7-ball near the top end rail.

#4 Reyes
16-5   **2-ball** C 1-rail outside draw.   **7H**
16-6   **3-ball** A 3-rails power draw/stun.   **8VH**
The lesson we just learned a moment ago is reinforced by Incardona's suggestion that Reyes could have knocked the 3-ball 2-rails near the 4-ball while pinning the cue ball behind the 8-ball. See **PYBNB 98**.
S/D/P Reyes shot on the 3-ball required an accurate and powerful stroke (speed) and the proper amount of draw to create the desired direction.

16-7   **4-ball** B 1-rail follow.   **3S**   **T:26**
Reyes didn't try to overplay the 4-ball. Instead he balanced his shot selection by shooting softly, following Principle #8. **PYBNB 150**.

Announcers Discussion There was a discussion about the problem a ball presents when it is frozen to the rail near the side pocket. See **PYBNB 150**.

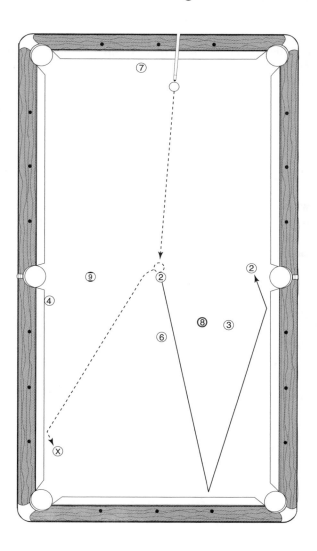

Amateur Play An alternative is to cut the 4-ball slightly on the right side with draw and float the cue ball behind the 9-ball. Even if you miss the hook, the 4-ball should be on or near the end rail if your speed is good.

16-8 **6-ball A+** 2-rails follow. **9EH   T:11**
The degree of difficulty is about a 9.8! Set it up and try it yourself. Reyes took only 11 seconds to prepare for this monumental shot.
P/S The direction of the cue ball takes care of itself on this shot. The main thing is pocketing the ball with an extremely hard stroke using inside english. Reyes hit the bulls eye in a tiny position zone.

SloMo This spectacular shot is worth several viewings. Reyes stayed locked in position until the cue ball had contacted the 6-ball.

16-9   **7-ball B** 1 rail follow. **5M**

PATTERN No Rails or Three?
Reyes complicated matters by playing for side pocket shape on the 8-ball. He could have used less speed on the 7-ball and sent the cue ball directly at the 8-ball, setting up a stop shot.

16-10 **8-ball B** 3 rails follow. **6MH**
16-11 **9-ball** 5D draw. **3S**

Between Racks
Discussion: **Bill Incardona** on the wearing effect of always being behind the whole way.
Reyes leads 9-7.

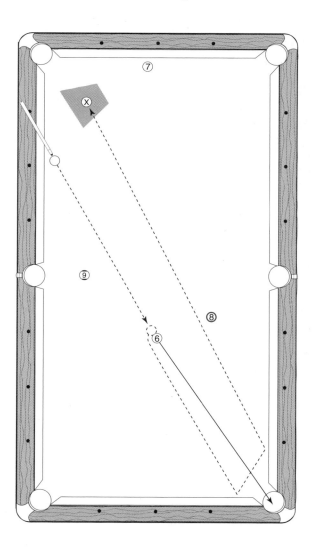

Game 17   Archer's Steel Trap
4 Inn.   TT4:02
#1 Reyes Breaks: Reyes made nothing.

#2 Archer
17-1   Safety 2VS
Archer played a safe and hooked Reyes. He also broke a cluster, setting up a run out. This strategic gem demonstrates the thinking of top players, who have minds like steel traps. Archer displayed a very fine touch as he hit the cue ball hard enough to avoid a foul while keeping it from peeking out from behind the 6-ball. This soft touch safety is tougher than it looks.

Incardona *"Nothing really gets by these players. They look over the table. They see where the problem area is and they feel that if I can deal with this problem area, if I can eliminate this problem then I can win this particular rack."*

#3 Reyes
17-2   Kick 7H
Reyes kicked into the 1-ball and scratched.
Reyes played a superb kick shot here, contacting the 1-ball thinly and sending the cue ball up table, possibly to a hook. He was a little unlucky to scratch. However, the cue ball was going to travel towards the area of the side pocket if played the way Reyes played it. There was at least a 25% chance of scratching on a well-executed safety. Reyes only took a scant 9 seconds preparing for

this shot. If he had surveyed the table from the bottom end rail, he would have seen the high-risk alleyway to the side pocket.

> *LESSON* **Mental Game** Sometimes you'll get a poor result on a well-executed shot. This often happens on shots that are impossible to gauge with far less than 100% accuracy. Such was the case with Reyes' kick shot. When a skillfully executed shot meets with disaster, you've got to regroup and get mentally prepared for your next turn. While in the chair take some solace in the fact you played the shot well. You should start looking over the table so you'll be ready in case your opponent fails to run out.

The Layout: B
The balls are spread widely across the table. There are no major problems, but rather a series of shots that are a little above average in difficulty. Getting on the 5-ball is a little tricky. And you must always be careful when planning for balls in the middle, such as the 7 and 8-balls.

"Johnny's going to be rewarded for a very excellent safety." **Maddux**

#4 Archer BIH
17-3　　**1-ball** C 1-rail follow.　　**3S**　　**T:17**
Archer placed the cue ball about seven inches from the 1-ball.
17-4　　**2-ball** C 1-rail follow.　　**5M**
17-5　　**3-ball** C 2-rails follow across.　　**5M**
17-6　　**4-ball** B+ 2-rails draw outside.　　**5M**

This shot shows the pinpoint control of a champion. Archer's cueing was extremely precise on this shot. A little more or less draw and he would have run into the 5-ball.

D/S Archer needed good direction to avoid hitting the 5-ball and adequate speed to land on the other side of the 5-ball.

_17-7_   **5-ball** B 2-rails inside follow.   **6MH**
See **PYBNB 94.**
S The key is hitting the cue ball hard enough to get an angle on the correct side of the 6-ball.

PATTERN Setting up a Ball in the Middle
Archer's main challenge was setting up the 6-ball properly to get on the 7-ball. The shot on the 5-ball sent the cue ball at Position A for a natural two-rail route from the 6-ball to the 7-ball. See Principle 14, **PYNBN 162.**

_17-8_   **6-ball** B 2-rails outside follow.   **5M   T:20**
Incardona felt Archer got on the wrong side of the 6-ball at Position A. Archer played down the line position for the 7-ball which is in the middle of the table. For another example of playing position on a ball in the middle of the table, see **PYBNB 211.**
The route to the 7-ball is shorter on the other side at Position B. However, this is one of those position plays where either side of the ball works just fine.

SloMo Note Archer's bridging technique on this awkward rail shot.

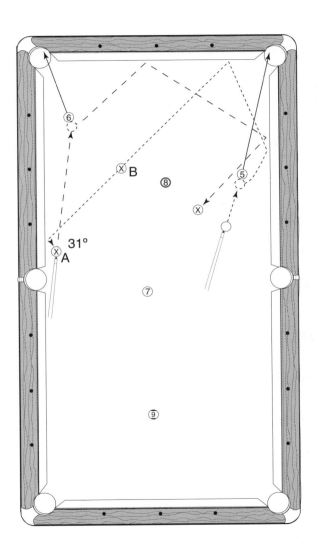

17-9   **7-ball** C 0-rail draw. **5M**

PATTERN When a Small Angle is Best
Archer obtained a 7-degree cut angle on the 7-ball
at Position A. This rather shallow cut angle was
perfect for sliding the cue ball over to Position B
for the 8-ball.

LESSON When you are playing position on balls
in the middle of the table, more often than not you
are better off with a shallow cut angle as this
makes it easier to control the cue ball. This is especially true when you are not going to be sending
the cue ball off a rail for position.

17-10   **8-ball** B 2-rails across follow. **6MH**
Archer executed a precise cross table route. Notice
the cue ball traveled towards the 9-ball after
bouncing off the left side rail.

LESSON Notice Archer's bridging technique. He
prefers a shorter bridge with his hand on the cloth
while Reyes, in this position, would normally use a
long rail bridge. Different rail bridges for different
folks.

17-11   **9-ball** Stop, 1-rail float. **6MH**

Reyes leads 9-8

Between Games: While Archer was on break,
Reyes was hitting the cue ball firmly down the
table. What was this all about? An exercise to stay
loose? Inquiring minds want to know.

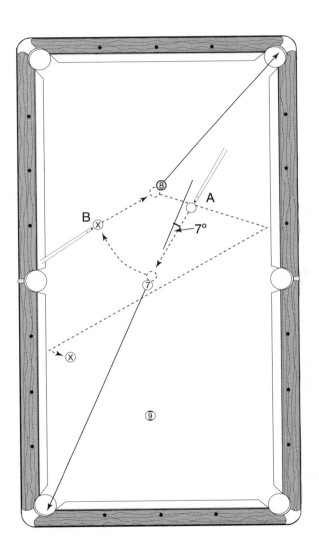

Game 18 Clutch Run Ties Score
1 Inn. TT6:02

#1 Archer Breaks: Archer made the 5-ball. The 5-ball was a hard earned ball as it wobbled in the side pocket, another sign that Archer's break was not very productive.

The Layout: A
A lot of B rated shots. There is nothing especially hard about any shot, but when you add up a series of moderately difficult position plays, you have a tough run. Position from the 3-ball to the 4-ball is the big key. You will notice there are a number of shots on which Archer took plenty of time in the preparation phase of the shot cycle.

18-1   **1-ball** B+ 3-rails follow.   **5M   T:26**
Archer propelled the cue ball 11' to Position A. The cue balls in Positions B and C show the challenging shots Archer would have faced if he had come up either a foot long or short of perfect. See **PYBNB 65** on the primary emphasis and Principle #1, **PYBNB 138-139**.
S/D This across the line position play required near perfect speed control. The three-rail route was very well played.

18-2   **2-ball** B 1-rail draw.   **6MH   T:29**
SloMo This draw shot gives you a good view of how the cue ball curves shortly after contact on an angled draw shot.

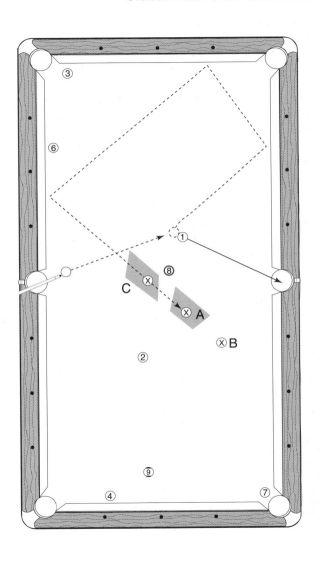

PATTERN Archer Succeeds His Way

I agree with the announcers that Archer's shot on
the 2-ball made the run more difficult. After the 2-
ball he played the route from Position A to the
shape zone. In doing so he violated Principles #4
(145), #12 (158), and #15 (162) **PYBNB**. Archer got
position anyway thanks to his perfect speed control on the 3-ball. With the cue ball in Position B,
Archer could have safely played down the line
shape on the 4-ball and eliminated the risk of getting hooked.

18-3   **3-ball** B 1-rail follow. **3S   T:22**
S Speed was everything on this shot: too short and
he's behind the 8-ball (sorry about that). Too long
and Archer's blocked by the 9-ball.

18-4   **4-ball** B+ 2-rails follow. **5M   ET:7**
P/D/S Proper cueing helped send the cue ball on a
journey straight up and down the table. Good
speed ensured that it bounced far enough off the
end rail for the 6-ball.

LESSON Archer showed how to go to the end rail
and out for position. This is usually much better
than babying the ball off one rail.

18-5   **6-ball** C 1-rail draw. **6MH**

SloMo This gives a good view of Archer's stroke
including his elbow drop on the follow through.

18-6   **7-ball** C 1-rail follow. **3S**
The 7-ball with a partial mistake because the 8-
ball was far from a routine shot.

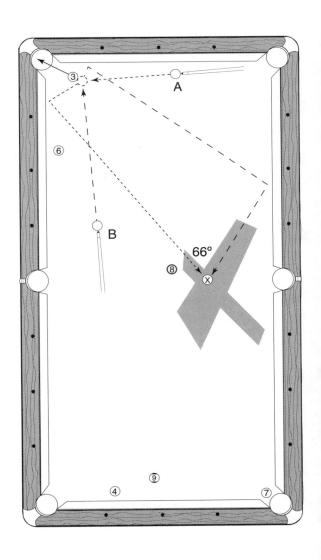

_18-7_   **8-ball** B 1-rail draw.   **6MH**   **T:48**
Archer took a full 48 seconds preparing himself for
this clutch shot.

Announcers Discussion
Incardona gave a good explanation of why Archer
played the 8-ball in the corner instead of the side.
Rewind and listen closely.

LESSON You should try to match your skills to
the shot at hand. In this example, Archer played
the more difficult shot on the 8-ball into the far
corner pocket. A less proficient shotmaker who is
skilled at position play would probably chose the
side pocket.

_18-8_   **9-ball** 1-rail follow, 15-degrees.   **3S**

Announcers Between Games There is an
enlightening discussion of Archer's task of coming
from behind. Maddux mentions the possibility of
Archer suffering an emotional letdown after strug-
gling to pull even. Incardona counters that this is
not likely:

_"Archer has the credentials to prove he never lets
up."_ **Incardona**

LESSON   **Mental Game** The Let Down
Syndrome is common among many amateur players and even a few pros. Remember: your task is
not complete until you have won the match. Keep
forging ahead with all you've got.

Score tied 9-9.

Game 19   Pocketing Error Costly
6 Inn.   TT8:25

#1 Archer Breaks: Archer made nothing.

Archer used 11 warm up strokes on this break, or 2 above his average, signaling how critical this shot was at this point in the match.

#2 Reyes

19-1   Bank Shot   7H   ET:7

Reyes missed a long rail bank. Earlier in the match Reyes fired away at a bank, made it, and won. Again he chose an aggressive shot, but missed, leaving Archer with a chance to gain control of the table.

***LESSON* #1** Certain aggressive shots look great when they go, but if they are near certain sellouts if missed, perhaps a more conservative shot is the better option. Shots like this are the kind you play when: 1) you're in peak form, 2) you are a skilled shotmaker, 3) you are behind and are trying to ignite your offense in the earlier stages of a match, or 4) your opponent is not a threat to run out.

***LESSON* #2** Most amateurs in Reyes' position would be much better off pushing out. Roll the cue ball two to three inches to the left and see if your opponent takes the bait. If they don't, you're now in a position to play a safety.

#3 Archer
19-2 Safety 3S

Archer played a safe, hooking Reyes. Archer bare-ly missed banking in the 1-ball. If he had made the 1-ball, it appears he would not have had much of a shot on the 2-ball.

#4 Reyes
19-3 Kick 9EH

Reyes kicked 1-rail, hit the 1-ball, but scratched. Reyes' most likely choice was to kick to pocket the 1-ball in the side. If so, he missed his contact point badly. This shows that kick shots are not easy even for the best kicker in the world.

The Layout: B
The tough part is getting from the 2 to the 3-ball. The rack is routine from the 4 through 9-balls.

#5 Archer BIH
19-4 1-ball B 0-rail draw. **6MH** **T:48**
Announcers Discussion: Incardona and Maddux debate playing a billiard or combo on the 3-ball.

LESSON Amateurs should consider sending the 1-ball down near the 2-ball as shown while locking the cue ball up behind the 9-ball. This strategy is especially potent if their opponent is poor at the kicking game. This shot eliminates the chance or running into the 8-ball when playing the 1-ball. With ball in hand it would then make is much eas-ier to get perfect shape on the 3-ball after pocket-ing the 2-ball. See **PYBNB 326.**

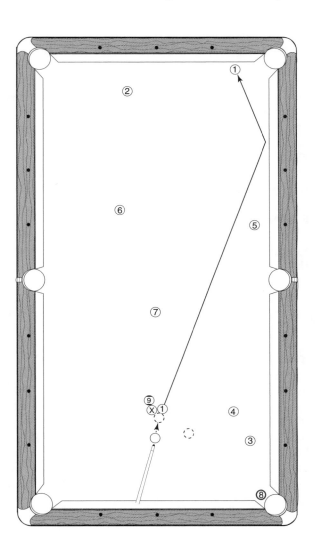

19-5 **2-ball** B 2-rails follow. **4MS** **T:21**
Archer was forced to play shape on the 3-8 billiard as the layout really offered no alternative approach.

SloMo Archer use five very short warm up strokes which mirrored his final stroke of about two inches on this delicate cut shot.

19-6 **8-ball** C 1-rail follow. **2VS** **T:52**
Archer took a long time setting up for this shot. He was undoubtedly well aware of the risk involved.

SloMo Notice the excellent close up view of this delicate shot. If Archer had hit the 4-ball just a little fuller, the cue ball would have hit further up the rail before contacting the 3-ball, enabling it to escape the jaws after contact. A fuller hit, however, would have knocked the 3-ball further from the rail. Archer hit the 8-ball nearly full, which was why the cue ball ended up in the jaws.

19-7 **3-ball** C 1 rail follow. **4MS** **T:21**
Archer's pocketing mistake cost him the game. The awkward bridge that resulted from Archer hitting the billiard incorrectly on the previous shot probably lead to his over cutting the 3-ball. Even though Archer made the 3-ball, the resulting path led to a hook behind the 7-ball.
D Notice after the shot that Archer pointed to a spot on the left side rail about five inches below where the cue ball struck the cushion.

LESSON Be sure on certain shots to make the ball in the correct part of the pocket, especially when the object ball is close to the pocket.

19-8 Kick Shot 8VH Archer kicked 3-rails and hit the 4-ball, leaving Reyes a tough shot.

LESSON Archer used his cue, as he often does, to line up a kick shot. Your cue can be an effective tool in planning your shots.

Layout: A
Reyes was faced with what turns out to be a series of demanding shots. The 4-ball is a very difficult shot, which makes getting perfect on the 5-ball a challenge. Once you get slightly out of line, a rack can play tough the rest of the way. It is a testament to Reyes' great skill that he was able to work his way through this rack.

#6 Reyes
19-9 4-ball A 1-rail draw. **6MH**
See **PYBNB 84.**
S/D If the cue ball had traveled another four to five inches, Reyes would not have had to elevate for the 5-ball, which made the 5-ball a much tougher shot. Still, the 4-ball was a very fine shot. The direction was superb thanks to Reyes' correct use of draw and outside (right) english.

19-10 5-ball B 1-rail draw. **5M**
SloMo This shot shows the importance of pocket-ing in position play. If you slow down the tape, you'll see that the 5-ball went in the far left side of

the pocket. This increased the cut angle and the cue ball's speed coming off the rail, which is why Reyes almost scratched in the left side pocket.

19-11   **6-ball** B+ 0-rail draw/stun.   **7H   T:20**

"If he's trying to make this particular game suspenseful, he's certainly doing his job." **Incardona**

19-12   **7-ball** B 1-rail draw.   **3S**
When the balls are within a few inches of each other, aiming can be a real challenge. Since the balls were so close together, a soft stroke was all that was required. A soft stroke on a cut shot with this angle results in contact throw of about 6-degrees, which must be allowed for. This shot demonstrated Reyes' delicate touch.

19-13   **9-ball** 0-rail stop.   **5M**

Reyes took a 10-9 lead, first to the hill.

Between Games: *"The fans are getting their money's worth to be sure."* **Maddux**

LESSON This exciting duel is building towards a grand conclusion, like a great symphony. When you are in a similar situation and you feel the excitement that comes with a close match, you must remind yourself to relax. Take some deep breaths and play each shot one at a time. Learn to relish a close match, cause that's what the game is really all about.

Game 20 Big Pressure Shot
2 Inn.   TT3:47

#1 Reyes Breaks: Reyes made nothing.

Incardona called out the break as three balls barely missed going in. Reyes was a bit unlucky, especially since one or more balls had fallen on seven of his nine previous break shots.

The Layout: B
The 1-ball was the first big key to this rack, especially considering the pressure Archer was under, trailing 9-10 in a race to 11. The rest of the rack is fairly routine except for the 5-ball, which is the next big key to running out. Archer's pace of play slowed substantially on this rack and during the final game.

#2 Archer
20-1   **1-ball** A 1-rail draw, long.   **7H   T:29**
SloMo This was an excellent shot considering survival in the match and the tournament was on the line. But this kind of cleanly pocketed ball is what you come to expect from one of the best players in the planet in the heat of big time competition against a world class opponent.

"The big problem was pocketing the one."
Incardona

20-2   **2-ball** C 0-rail draw.   **6MH   T:21**

PATTERN Close Up Straight In Position

Archer played the 2 through 4-balls like a Nine Ball player, using angles and the rails for position. This series of shots, however, could have been played with a series of short-range draw shots (in the style of a superb 14.1 player), which would have greatly minimized cue ball movement.

S The shot on the 2-ball was all about draw speed control. Archer drew back to Position A for the 3-ball. If he had drawn back to Position B, he could have then drawn back to Position C for the 4-ball. Finally, an eight inch draw shot on the 4-ball would have given him the ideal angle for playing the 5-ball in the lower left corner pocket.

LESSON Archer surveyed the table (see **PYNBN 148**) after playing the 2-ball to see if the 5-ball would pass the 9-ball. This was a good idea, but he should have surveyed the layout before playing the 2-ball, as it could have affected his decision making for the sequence of shots that followed.

20-3 **3-ball** C 1-rail draw. **5M**
Archer applied a little too much draw on the 3-ball. If he had played the 3-ball correctly, he could have avoided going to the end rail and out when playing the 4-ball.

20-4 **4-ball** B 1-rail draw. **6MH**
See **PYBNB 87.**
Archer recovered position nicely for the 5-ball.

20-5 **5-ball** B 3-rails draw. **7H**
On this classic 3-rail position play Archer came up a little short. This was a very minor error considering how well Archer got on the 7-ball.

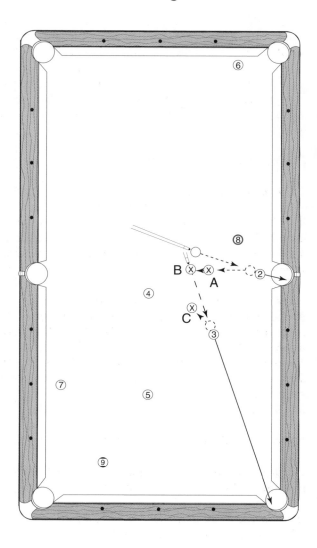

LESSON I hope I'm not offending anyone here, but I simply must point out that I've seen so many amateur players go for combos like the 5-9 when the run out is fairly routine. If the combo in this position does happen to give you a better chance of winning the game, either your position play needs some serious work or you are perhaps the world's best at combos.

20-6   **6-ball** B 2-rails follow.   **4MS**

LESSON Archer used a short stroke for this rail shot. The short stroke increases your accuracy and it eliminates any tendency to use excessive power. Even though Reyes might use a long bridge and lengthy stroke, in this position, the short stroke is recommended for most players.

20-7   **7-ball** C 1-rail draw.   **5M**
Archer had an ideal angle on this shot to cross the table for the 8-ball. See Principle #2, **PYBNB 142**.
20-8   **8-ball** C 0-rail draw.   **6MH**
Archer wisely avoided overplaying this shot. He drew back about a foot, accepting a slightly longer shot on the 9-ball.
20-9   **9-ball** 20-degrees 2-rails draw.   **7H**

Score is tied at 10-10. Double Hill.

Between Games Archer performs a rack inspection and gets Reyes to rerack the balls.

"Double hill, you gotta love it." **Maddux**
"Somebody's gotta go." **Incardona**

Game 21 "Give Me a Menu"
13 Inn. TT20:36

This titanic duel lasted 13 innings and contained some of the finest defensive play you'll ever see. And to top if off, Incardona was in dead punch on the mike. Enjoy!!!

Technique Archer took a full 25 seconds staring at the break end of the table before coming to a decision on where he wanted to break the balls. He was able to make a ball and gain control of the table, so the extra effort was time well spent.

#1 Archer Breaks: Archer made the 7-ball.
21-1 **2-ball** B+ 2-rail. **8VH T:59 ET:7**
A pound shot on combo with no position.
21-2 **Safety 2VS**
Archer played a safe (or missed a tough side pocket shot because of a skid, as Incardona noted). He hooked Reyes.

#2 Reyes
21-3 **Kick Shot 4MS**
Reyes kicked 1 rail and hit, leaving the edge of the 1-ball. Diagrammed in **PYBNB 348.**

"From the position he was in, he did exactly what he had to do." **Incardona**

As Archer spends some time looking over a shot, Incardona muses:
"If we run out of tape I'm just going to cry." **Incardona**

Note: This production was truly blessed: the tape was changed just a moment before Archer pulled the trigger on a crucial safety.

#3 Archer
21-4 **Safety 4MS ET:7**
Archer hit the 1-ball a little too fully on his safety attempt, leaving Reyes a tough shot. If he had hit the 1-ball thinner, the cue ball would have traveled to the far end rail. See **PYBNB 283.**

LESSON There is a tendency to hit the object ball too thickly on long distance thin cut safeties. This is caused by the fear of missing the ball entirely. Should you: 1) take a chance on playing a great thin hit safety, possibly giving your opponent ball in hand if you miss the ball, or 2) bail out and hit the ball too fully, which often results in a playable shot or return safety for your opponent? I would advise that you put your ego aside, risk looking foolish, and go for the thin hit. You either execute a safety correctly or you don't.

#4 Reyes
21-5 **Misses 4MS ET:7**
He missed a tough shot and left a hit.

SloMo You'll see Reyes jump up well before the cue ball hits the 1-ball.

Tip: Try shooting moderately difficult 30-40 degree cut shots with the object ball near the middle of the table. After pocketing several in succession, shoot a few where you purposefully start to jump up a split second before contact.

If you should happen to start missing, take notice of where the object ball hits the rail. When playing a match, if you start to miss to the same side of the pocket, this could be sign you are not staying down on your shots.

#5 Archer
21-6 Safety **3S**

Archer played a safety but hit the ball a bit too thinly, leaving Reyes a long shot or safety. See **PYBNB 280.**

LESSON Hooking via this 2-rail route is a vital skill. Tip: Set up this shot and try to send the cue ball behind the blocker. Use the donuts (three hole reinforcements) so you can play the exact same shot until you've got it mastered. Observe the cue ball's path as you change the thickness of the hit on the object ball. Also observe how changes in your tip position affect the cue ball's path.

#6 Reyes
21-7 Safety **2VS**

Reyes could have jacked up a little and played the 1-ball in the upper left corner pocket. Instead, he chose to played safe, hooking Archer behind the 6-ball.

LESSON Pros play the percentages by routinely passing on difficult shots in favor of a safety. In the same spot, many amateurs first impulse is to go for the shot. This is caused by: 1) a desire to impress the crowd (ego), 2) they are offensive oriented (their game is out of balance) or 3) they may not see the safety (lack of knowledge).

#7 Archer
21-8 Kick Shot 6MH

Archer kicked 3-rails and hit, hooking Reyes This awesome shot saved the match for Archer. The crowds erupted! This shot is an exquisite blend of skill and luck, as is the case with difficult kick shots that turn out this well.

LESSON Archer took 74 seconds studying this shot before taking his stance. You might feel uncomfortable holding up play this long to ponder your options. On key shots where the match is on the line, however, you can and should make an exception. Take as much time as you need (within reason, of course) to sift through your options. Then make a firm decision, commit to a course of action, and then give it your best shot.

#8 Reyes
21-9 Kick 4MS

He kicked 1-rail and hooked Archer.

Announcer Discussion Rewind and listen to Incardona's gems. They're the best!

Incardona in Dead Stroke in the Booth

"What kind of wizardry are we about to see here?"

"Give me a menu and let me order. Let me order something from the menu. I'll order a kick two-cushion hook safety."

"Now does the good doctor have a prescription for this."

"It takes players like this to sustain the suspense."

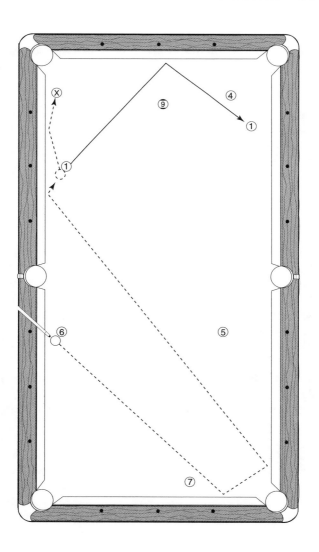

#9 Archer
21-10 **Kick Shot 7H**
He kicked 1-rail and into a long rail bank and
pocketed the 1-ball!!

21-11 **Safety 4MS**
Archer's safety hooked Reyes. This routine bank
safety made full use of the 3 and 9-balls as blockers. It also used distance as a strategic weapon.
See **PYBNB 312.**

*"Now that shot was hard to describe. Just think
about how hard it would be to execute."* **Incardona**
on the shot Reyes is about to play.

#10 Reyes
21-12 **Kick Shot 7H ET:7**
Reyes kicked 2-rails, hit the correct portion of the 3-
ball, and gave himself a chance to get a good break,
which is what happened when he hooked Archer.
See a similar kick on page **351, PYBNB**.

#11 Archer
21-13 **Kick/Rail First 4MS**
Archer played a rail first two-way shot and missed,
but left Reyes hooked. Note that he played the
shot with his cue level.

LESSON This is a shot where many amateurs
might bemoan their bad luck at being hooked and
simply slam into the ball off the end rail while hop-
ing for the best. Top pros, however, carefully study
their options and look for the optimal shot or
strategy.

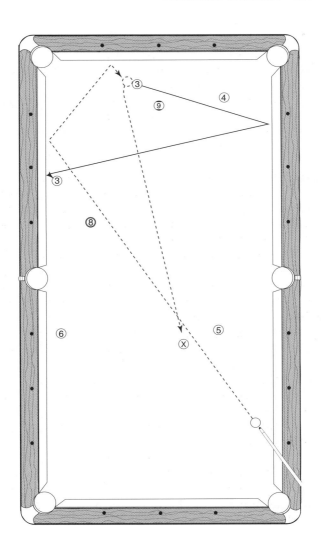

#12 Reyes
21-14   **Kick Shot   8VH**

Reyes kicked three rails and hit, leaving Archer a shot. He barely missed. A single solitary inch is the margin of victory and defeat!

Observe Reyes walking from the table with a good natured look of bemusement, knowing that he probably just got knocked out of the tournament. He is a true gentleman.

LESSON A year earlier in the finals of the Sands 21 tournament, Reyes made one of the most astounding kick shots in the history of the game in the 25th game to nip Earl Strickland at the wire 13-12. Diagrammed in **PYBNB 343**.

If Reyes had pocketed the kick shot in the illustration, the crowd would have gone nuts, he would almost certainly have run out, and the announcers would have would have expounded on Reyes' legendary kicking skills.

The kicking game, as I've mentioned several times before, is a fickle blend of skill and luck. Like putting in golf, sometimes a well-played shot is destined for the pocket and at others the pool gods have simply determined it is not your time to win. So enjoy you successful kicks, but learn to accept the near misses as Reyes did, for they will always be a part of the game.

Announcers Discussion Incardona gave a classic talk on how tired Archer must be at this point in the match, as he had to weather Reyes' onslaught of kicks and safeties.

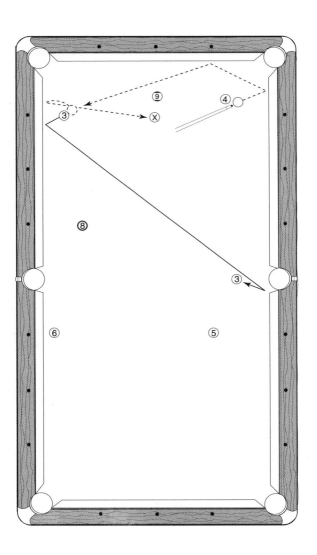

The Layout: C
This is a routine out. Position from the 5-ball to the 6-ball is the key. However, under the pressure of double hill, it might rate an A in difficulty.

#13 Archer
21-15 **3-ball** C 1-rail follow.   **4MS**
SloMo Observe closely the path of the cue ball after contact. The follow caused the cue ball to bend just in time or else it would have crashed into the 5-ball as Maddux exclaimed.

"If he gets out here, trust me, it's a lot more difficult than it looks." **Incardona**

21-16 **4-ball** C 1-rail follow.   **4MS**   **T:46**

PATTERN Alternate Route Lowers Risk
Archer Played shape on the 6- ball from Position A. The diagram shows an alternate approach that takes the side pocket or a possible hook behind the 8-ball out of play. This may be preferable for those who lack Archer's control. Use a quarter tip of right english when playing the 4-ball so the cue ball ends up at Position B. The 14-degree cut angle is perfect for playing a stun shot, which would send the cue ball to Position C for the 6-Ball.

21-17 **5-ball** B 2-rails draw. **8VH**   **T:23**
Archer used the principles of Allowing for a Margin for Error (**PYBNB 145**) and Avoiding a Scratch (**PYBNB 165**) in executing this superb position play.
D The key was to control the direction and avoid a side pocket scratch or hook behind the 8-ball.

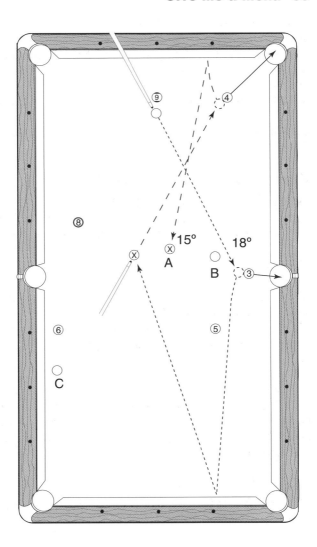

21-18 **6-ball** B 0-rail draw. **4MS** **T:23**
21-19 **8-ball** C 1-rail follow. **4MS**
The 8-ball went in the right side of the pocket. This pocketing error is why the cue ball ended up near the rail.
21-20 **9-ball** 0-rail follow. **3S**

SloMo Watch the 9-ball as it enters the pocket. It does the left-right-left and in.

Post Game Comments
"Here's Bill and Johnny"
"Anybody who buys this tape should call Pat up and say I owe you more for this." **Incardona**

"What a match." **Incardona**

"He was worn, totally worn and it showed. But he was able to get the job done."
"Quite honestly it is probably the most suspenseful game I've ever had the pleasure of watching."
Bill Incardona

"I didn't want to say do I have the strength to get out. Well do I have the strength to make the first ball and do I have the strength to make the second ball. That's the only way I can view the whole table.
Johnny Archer

"My toughest opponent is myself."
Johnny Archer

Part II
Capelle on the Pro Game

Introduction

Most serious fans would agree that Johnny Archer and Efren Reyes are two of the very finest 9-ball players ever. In fact, both are a lock for the BCA Hall of Fame. It follows that the majority of what we will be discussing about these players will be focused on what they do correctly. Nevertheless, they are human and do, on occasion, make errors in judgment and/or execution, just like anyone else. So it is with all due respect and admiration for them as players, and ambassadors of the game, that I will point out mistakes and deficiencies in their games so that you, as a student of the game, can derive maximum value from my findings.

My analysis is based on their games as they stood in 1996. It is possible that either player may have changed their style somewhat since then. To accumulate the data on which the research is based, I viewed the match over 10 times. Each viewing was punctuated with numerous interruptions as I replayed shots, listened to the announcers, made diagrams, timed shots, and recorded my observations. I feel confident in the accuracy of the information and conclusions you are about to read due to my intensive study of the match. My findings are meant to add to your understanding of what it takes to play pool at a very high level. They may also serve as a source for lively debate about the pros and cons of each player's method of play.

How to Use Part II

In upcoming sections are numerous tables and charts that illuminate the performances of Archer and Reyes and that showcase their skills. I have analyzed the data and come to many conclusions that can help you improve your game. You will also find several lists of shots in various categories that are worth further study. At the end of each section is a summary called **Your Game** with advice you can easily incorporate into your game. If you are not into the detailed statistics and analysis, you may wish to confine your study to these sections.

There are many elements that make up a complete game of pool. It takes time to fully develop each skill. I suggest that you develop a systematic game plan for practicing and improving your game. For further information on how to structure your practice sessions please see pages 397-407 of **PYBNB**.

Summaries
A Duel for the Ages

The match between Archer and Reyes took place at The Sands 23, June 1996 in Reno, Nevada. At that time they were the two top ranked players in the world. Both the fans and announcers expected to see this match in the finals. However, this losers bracket match would eliminate one player from the competition with a 9-12th place finish. The summary will give you a feel for the ebb and flow of this tightly contested match between two great players.

Reyes Takes Command

Archer won the lag handily and opened the festivities with a break and run, demonstrating arguably the best break in pool. Archer's run was the first of eight game winning runouts that averaged an impressive 7.13 balls. After **Game 1**, Archer would never hold the lead again until the final game was over. After Game 1, he would be frustrated by his lack of productivity on the break.

Archer failed to make a ball on the break in **Game 2**, and Reyes made quick work of an easy layout. Reyes ran out three times after Archer came up empty on the break. Reyes' softer break was working quite well, but he never fully capitalized on it as he won only two one-inning games. The runout was the first of Reyes' nine gamewinning runouts, which averaged 7.22 balls.

Reyes broke and ran **Game 3** to take a 2-1 lead, but only after narrowly avoiding disaster on the 1-ball.

After committing a position error late in **Game 4**, Reyes unloaded a "Mike Massey" 3-rail draw shot on the 7-ball to grab a 3-1 advantage .

Reyes committed the first of six game losing errors in **Game 5** when he corner hooked himself on a difficult position play. Archer ultimately prevailed after much defensive play. Reyes led the game-losing mistakes category with six errors to Archers three. This one stat alone may have been the biggest key to Archer's victory.

Reyes quickly recovered from his mistake with an excellent run out in **Game 6**, which was keyed by his "field goal" position on the 2-ball. He snapped in the 9-ball in **Game 7** to take a three game lead, 5-2. This would be the largest gap as the rest of the match was a closely fought duel to the finish.

Archer Fights Back

Some players might weaken after their opponent had broken in the 9-ball to open a three game lead, especially when trailing a tough opponent. Archer, to his credit, stayed cool and pulled to within two games at 3-5 after a Reyes' miscue sent the cue ball flying off the table in **Game 8**.

Archer added another short rack victory in **Game 9**, pocketing a spectacular billiard to trail by a 4-5 margin. Reyes was a little unlucky because his safety preceding Archer's gamewinner missed by less than an inch of hooking Archer.

Reyes was cruising through a fairly routine run in **Game 10** when he hooked himself, giving Archer a chance to tie the score. But Archer failed to snooker Reyes on a routine safety and trailed once again by two games at 4-6. Reyes' four ball run included 3-rail position following a power cross side bank shot.

Reyes faced a tough layout following the break in **Game 11**. He committed a series of errors including a masse safety that virtually handed the game to Archer, who now trailed 5-6. In **Game 12**, the pool gods evened the count at 1-1 for 9-balls on the break, allowing Archer to momentarily tie the score at 6-6.

In **Game 13**, Archer once again failed to pocket a ball on the break. Reyes cashed in with his third and final second player run out, polishing off a relatively easy layout to take a slim 7-6 lead. Reyes extended his lead after **Game 14** to 8-6 thanks to a nifty two-way bank safety and a superb 3-rail position play on the 2-ball that set up an easy run out.

Now or Never

At this point, Archer's chances looked slim as he would have to now outscore Reyes 5-2 without his break working. In addition, since he had spent the majority of his time in the chair, (three of his six wins had come on short racks where he played a total of four shots) there was a chance he might now be out of stroke.

After the break, Reyes faced a difficult 4-rail around the table position play. He missed and scratched. Archer meticulously worked his way through a routine layout to capture **Game 15** and pull once again to within a game at 7-8. Reyes would establish a two game advantage in the next game. Nevertheless, his failure to run this rack enabled Archer to avoid a 6-9 deficit and near certain defeat.

Reyes, who is known as The Magician, put on a magical display of cue wizardry in **Game 16**, which was capped by a simply awesome long distance 2-rail position play off the rail which required an extremely hard stroke with inside english. Wow!! Reyes superlative effort earned him a two game lead at 9-7.

Setting the Table

In **Game 17** Reyes barely missed making a ball on the break. Archer then played a heads up safety, eliminating a trouble spot while he also hooked Reyes. Reyes quickly played a soft 2-rail kick shot but scratched in the side pocket. Archer ran out to pull within one game at 8-9. Archer then tied the score at 9-9 with a break and run of a challenging layout in **Game 18**, his first since the opening rack. The runout included a controversial pattern that could have resulted in disaster.

Archer, having clawed his way back into the match, had a golden opportunity in **Game 19** to reach the hill first after Reyes scratched on a kick shot for the third time in the match. However, Archer committed only his second serious position error of the match when a pocketing mistake led to a hook. Reyes then took command of a difficult layout to reach the hill first with a 10-9 lead.

In **Game 20** Reyes failed to make a ball on the break and Archer stepped to the table facing a long and difficult shot on the 1-ball and a 9-10 deficit. During the entire match, Archer had missed only one shot. Therefore, it was no surprise that he showed the heart of a champion, cleanly pocketing the shot. His subsequent run out set the stage for one of the most exciting and memorable double hill games ever played.

"Give Me a Menu"

Archer and Reyes put on a dazzling display of kick shots and safeties in **Game 21**. Reyes had an excellent opportunity to run out in the forth inning but missed a moderately difficult shot. After failing to hook Reyes in the fifth inning, Archer responded to a Reyes safety with a match saving 3-rail kick shot that drew a thunderous response from the crowd. Reyes countered with the hook safety that Incardona ordered up from the menu.

In the twelfth inning Reyes missed pocketing a kick shot by no more than an inch and Archer was able to struggle home with a six ball run out to claim victory. Archer would go on to finish second to Nick Varner after losing in the finals 9-11. Reyes ended up in the 9-12 slot in a select field of 58 of the world's best players.

Key Stats

The Score

Archer trailed 2-5 at one point, but outscored **Reyes** 9-5 from then on to take the match.

After Reyes tied the score by winning the second game, Archer never lead again until the final game.

Innings Summary

11 of the first 20 games were decided in one or two innings. The final game took 13 innings!

Key Mistakes

Archer won six games because of Reyes' mistakes.

Reyes won three games because of Archer's mistakes.

Advantage Archer.

The Rolls
Archer got the best of the rolls, probably about four ahead.

Run Out Opportunities
Archer converted 89% of his runout attempts to **Reyes'** 69%.

Reyes faced four layouts rated B+ or higher to only one for Archer.

Time of Possession
Archer was able to stay in stroke for a strong finish even though **Reyes** dominated table time with 76 shots to Archer's 30 over the first 14 games.

BIH Summary
Reyes committed six fouls to **Archers** one.

Break Analysis
Both players had losing records on their break. **Archer** was 5-6, while **Reyes** was 4-6 despite making at least one ball on 7 of 10 breaks.

Push Out Summary
There was only one push out. **Reyes**, the pusher, lost to **Archer's** spectacular billiard.

Shotmaking
Archer faced fewer tough shots than Reyes, but nevertheless shot with amazing accuracy, missing only a table length shot in Game 16.

Reyes was equally accurate on routine shots. His five misses came on a variety of challenging shots including a critical shot in the double hill game.

Safeties
Among the 19 safeties were only four that lead directly to a win, and four that lead immediately to a loss.

Kick Shots

Only four of fourteen kick shots resulted in a hook. **Reyes** scratched on three kick shots, but only lost two of those games. Reyes made contact on all nine of his kick shots. **Archer** missed contact on only one of six kick shots.

Game Summary
The Score Game by Game

After the match was tied following the second game, Archer played catch up for most of the remainder of the match. In fact, he only led after the first and last games. The announcers commented frequently on the score throughout the match and how Archer was always fighting an uphill battle. When Reyes snapped in the 9-ball to take a three game lead of 5-2, many players at that point would have weakened, but not Archer. Reyes held the lead after 15 games, but as they said in the movie "The Hustler", you "don't get paid for yardage." Archer came on with a flourish at the end, winning four of the last five games.

Lead/Defecit Game by Game

Archer	1	0	-1	-2	-1	-2	-3	-2	-1	-2
Game	1	2	3	4	5	6	7	8	9	10
Reyes	-1	0	1	2	1	2	3	2	1	2

Archer	-1	0	-1	-2	-1	-2	-1	0	-1	0	1
Game	11	12	13	14	15	16	17	18	19	20	21
Reyes	1	0	1	2	1	2	1	0	1	0	-1

A **RRR** A **RR** AA **R** AA **RR** A **R** AA **R** AA

Your Game: The Effect of the Score

Try to never let the score affect the quality of your play. It's nice to have a lead, and it's not much fun to be behind. But in the final analysis, you've simply got to play pool no matter who is your opponent or whatever the score.

Innings Summary

The pros cherish every turn at the table. They know their opponent will not often relinquish control of the table without a fight. The average game lasted 3.38 turns, but only because of Game 21, which took 13 innings. This figure is in line with my 500 Game Study in which the average game, when played from the break box, lasted 3.27 innings. Games in which the players could break anywhere lasted an average of 2.93 turns.

Total Innings
71 innings = 3.38 per game
Innings by Game:
1 2 1 5 8 2 1 4 3 4 2 1 2 3 2 4 4 1 6 2 13
Summary
A The match was an interesting blend of short rack wins, long run outs, and defensive battles.
B Four of the games went five innings or more.
C The first 20 games were decided in an average of 2.9 turns.
D The last game, which was a 13-inning defensive gem, brought the average of the match to 3.38
E 11 of the 21 games, or 52.4%, were decided in one or two innings.
F This 52.4% average coincides closely with the 53.6% recorded in my 500 Game Study.

Innings Per Game

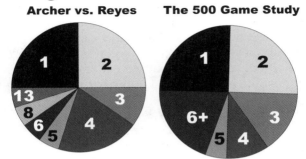

Archer vs. Reyes   The 500 Game Study

Your Game: Value Each Turn

I've witnessed amateur players take a cavalier attitude towards far too many of their turns at the table. While you may get by with this approach at a certain level of play, it will simply not work as you progress up the competitive ladder. So make a habit of placing a higher value on each and every turn at the table. Play smart pool, don't just fire and hope for the best. Make your opponent work for everything. This approach stamps you as a serious competitor, and it can have a demoralizing effect on many players.

Whose Game?

In any match there are those games in which only one player has a legitimate chance to win. These kind of games include break and runs, run outs when the other player failed to make a ball on the break, 9-balls on the break, or safeties that lead to a win. In this match, Archer was the clear-cut winner in five games while seven games clearly belonged to Reyes.

Matches are often won by who is able to capture the majority of the games that are up for grabs. Nine games were up for grabs in this match. Six of these went to Archer and only three to Reyes. The table below shows where there was an obvious winner and the games that are up for grabs. The key mistake is highlighted in bold type.

	Winner	Whose Game	How Won or Lost
1	A	A	Break and runout.
2	R	R	Second player runout.
3	R	R	Break and runout.
4	R	??	Archer played a poor **safety**, and missed a kick shot.
5	A	??	Reyes **position error**. Archer used good strategy
6	R	R	Second player runout.
7	R	R	9-ball on break.
8	A	??	Reyes **miscued**, leaving Archer an easy combo.
9	A	??	Reyes **safety** left Archer a long billiard on the 9-ball.
10	R	??	Archer failed to hook on safety after a Reyes error.
11	A	??	Reyes lost **position**, and then played a poor safety.
12	A	A	9-ball on the break.
13	R	R	Second player runout.
14	R	R	Two-way shot after the break lead to a win.
15	A	??	Reyes **missed** and scratched Second player run out.
16	R	R	Reyes great runout (I can't fault Archer for missing a long shot.)

	Winner	Whose Game	How Won or Lost
17	A	A	Great safety.
18	A	A	Break and runout.
19	R	??	Archer made a **pocketing error** and got hooked.
20	A	A	Second player runout.
21	A	??	Up for grabs, but Reyes **missed** a shot to win.

Whose Game Summary

5 Archer's clear-cut wins.
7 Reyes' clear-cut wins.
9 up for grabs.

Turnovers That Led to Losses

Reyes 6
Archer 3

"Could Have" Score - Reverse the Outcome By Eliminating the Crucial Mistakes

This is purely theoretical, as the break would have switched over to the new winner.

Archer 11 -6 + 3 = 8
Reyes 10 -3 + 6 = 13

Your Game: Win "Your" Games

A proven formula for winning matches is to win the vast majority of games "you are supposed to win" and then capitalize on your opponents mistakes when they fail to put away the games "they are supposed to win". In short, limit your turnovers and capitalize on your opponent's errors. Be a pool opportunist!

The Rolls

The rolls are simply the breaks of the game, both the good and the bad. I took some liberties when evaluating the rolls as that is the nature of the beast. For example, some players might think Reyes getting hooked on the 5-ball in Game 10 was bad luck. However, I think it was just a poorly executed shot. Reyes would not have come close to getting hooked if he had hit the shot as intended. On the other hand, I felt he got a bad roll when he scratched on a superbly executed kick in Game 5. In my opinion, there were 10 shots in the match that qualified as bad rolls, or that were borderline. I would like to hear your opinion. Perhaps there are some shots you would add or subtract from my list after watching the tape. For more on the rolls, see page 185 of *A Mind For Pool*, page 347 of *Play Your Best Pool* and page 382 of *Play Your Best Nine Ball*.

Game 5
#7 The cue ball barely toppled in the side after Reyes played an excellent kick shot. If he had not scratched, he might have won the game.

Game 8
#3 Reyes got both a good and bad roll on the 1-ball. It was a good roll to avoid getting hooked behind the 3 and 9-balls, and a bad roll to tie up the balls.
#4 Archer got a good break to have an easy win handed to him.

Game 9
#2 Reyes came within less than an inch of hooking Archer after a fine safety attempt.

Game 17
#3 Reyes scratched after playing a fine kick shot.
Game 21
#7 Archer played a safe that was part skill, part luck.

#9 Archer made a lucky kick bank, which kept him from losing the game.

#10 Reyes kicked and hooked Archer. Part skill, part luck.

#11 Archer missed a rail first kick shot and hooked Reyes.

#12 Reyes barely missed making a kick shot. Bad luck?

Your Game: Accepting the Rolls
It certainly helps your cause when you are the recipient of a great break, or good roll. However, it is often your response to the bad breaks that determines how often you visit the winner's circle. While neither Archer nor Reyes certainly relished their bad luck, they stoically took their seat when they were the victim of misfortune. Their attitude serves to minimize the impact of the bad rolls. It also allows them to have the proper mindset for their next trip to the table. You're certainly going to get your share of the bad rolls along with the good. I therefore suggest you adopt a fatalistic or even bemused attitude towards the rolls.

Tip: If you don't cry about your bad rolls, after awhile it won't seem as if the rolls are so stacked against you.

Time of Possession

During the first 14 games, Reyes took 76 shots to Archer's 30 shots (all non-break shots) in building an 8-6 lead. Archer captured five of the last seven games, during which his shots out numbered Reyes' by a margin of 55 to 25.

One of the main ingredients to Archer's victory was his ability to deliver a strong closing performance after spending so much time in his chair in the early going.

Archers Shots	**Total**	**Average/Game**
Games 1-14	30	2.14
Games 15-21	55	7.86
Reyes Shots		
Games 1-14	76	5.43
Games 15-21	25	3.57

Your Game: Playing when Cold

Monopolizing the table in the early stages can help you get in stroke and give you momentum that can carry though to the end of a match. However, if you are a spectator in the beginning stages, you must still be able to bring your game to the table when you get a chance to shoot. This is more easily accomplished if you have solid fundamentals rather than a quirky style that needs to be constantly in use to gain peak efficiency.

Fundamentals

Bridges

The bridge is one of the foundations of a solid game. In the sections below are my results from counting the bridges used by Archer and Reyes. The figures are broken into four broad categories. Understand, however, that within each category are several minor variations. For example, not all of Archer's open bridges on the table are constructed exactly alike nor are all of Reyes closed rail bridges precisely the same.

The Four Basic Bridges

Closed Bridge

Reyes used the closed bridge (on the table) on 61.5% of his position plays. Archer used the closed bridge (on the table) on 31.5% of his position plays.

Open Bridge

The open bridge was used by both players for routine shots that required no more than a very soft to medium speed of stroke. An open bridge helps with soft shots requiring feel as it reduces friction between your bridge and the cue. An open bridge also gives you a better view of the cue ball, which helps aiming. Archer used the open bridge on 40.7% of his position plays. Reyes, in contrast, used the open bridge on only 10.8% of his position plays.

Closed Rail Bridge

When they must bridge on the rail, both players overwhelmingly prefer to use a closed rail bridge. And they make every effort to keep the cue as level as possible.

Open Rail Bridge

Both players use an open rail bridge only when the cue ball is very close to the rail. They were required to use the open rail bridge on only about 6% of all position plays. This is further evidence of their fine control of the cue ball.

Overall Bridge Usage

Type	Archer	%	Reyes	%
Closed	19	22.4	48	47.5
Open	35	41.2	13	12.9
Rail - Cl.	24	28.2	31	30.7
Rail - Op.	7	8.2	9	8.9
Total	**85**		**101**	

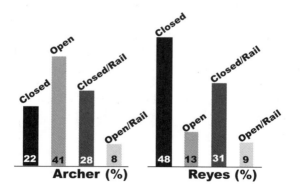

Bridging Technique
Bridge Basics
Archer and Reyes use bridges that allow them to keep their cue as level as possible, especially on rail shots. They also vary the length of their bridge slightly to match the speed of the shot. Long bridges are used for power shots and short bridges are employed for softer strokes.

Archer's Technique
Archer prefers an open bridge for most routine shots and follow shots. He uses a closed bridge for the majority draw shots and for power shots. He tends to use a bridge that's several inches shorter than Reyes' standard bridge.

Archer's shorter bridge length is recommended for most players who do not have the time or talent to master the considerably longer stroke preferred by Reyes.

Reyes Technique
Reyes prefers a closed bridge for the vast majority of shots when bridging on the cloth. Reyes uses a long bridge for most shots, which enables him to keep his cue as level as possible. He also uses a closed bridge because it adds stability to his long bridge.

Reyes uses a long closed bridge while cueing very low. This gives him a great view of the cue ball, which assists in aiming. Reyes' method requires you to strike the cue ball in a place other than your setup position. This technique is not easily mastered.

Reyes tip contacts the cue ball at a shallower angle than most players on draw shots because of his long bridge. This reduces the masse effect on mishits. The long bridge, however, magnifies any sideways movement in your stroke.

Reyes often uses a stroke that's not nearly as long as his rail bridge. This indicates that the long bridge is for comfort and/or sighting, not for a long power stroke.

Position Play Bridge Summary

The summary below shows how often Archer and Reyes wind up with a rail shot when they are playing position. Most rail shots from playing position are due to the layout more than positional errors. This theory is supported by the very few instances when either player left himself with the cue ball frozen or within an inch or two of the rail.

The study does not include the first shot of a run because the bridge used for that shot resulted from an opponent's shot or the break, not from playing position. Ball-in-hand first shots of a run are also not included because the player did not have to achieve position from playing a shot. The study does include shots on the 9-ball.

Bridges from Playing Position

Type	Archer	%	Reyes	%
Closed	17	31.5	40	61.5
Open	22	40.7	7	10.8
Rail - Cl.	12	22.2	14	21.5
Rail - Op.	3	5.6	4	6.2

The table below shows the kind of bridges that result when your opponent controls your shot via, for example, a safety or kick shot, or when you are not executing a position play. After comparing it to the table above, you can see that rail bridges are much more commonly used under these circumstances.

Bridges Used After the Break

Type	Archer	%	Reyes	%
Closed	2	6.5	8	22.2
Open	13	42.1	6	16.7
Rail - Cl.	12	40.7	17	47.2
Rail - Op.	4	12.9	5	15.2
Total	**31**		**36**	

The table below demonstrates that both players were about dead even when it came to playing position off the rail and on the table.

Table Versus Rail Bridges on Position Play

Bridge	Archer	%	Reyes	%
Table	39	72.2	47	72.3
Rail	15	27.8	18	27.7

On the Rail Percentages

	Table		Rail	
	#	%	#	%
Position	86	72.3	33	27.7
Overall	115	61.8	71	38.2

Your Game: Learn to Play off the Rail
All pool players are counseled early in their careers to keep the cue ball away from the rails. Nevertheless, two of the best players in the world still played nearly 28% of their position plays from the rail and over 38% of their shots overall using a rail bridge. The very obvious conclusion is that you had better become proficient at shooting off the

rails, and that you should master a variety of closed rail bridges.

Use a Variety of Bridge Lengths

I advise you to use a variety of bridge lengths. Use a short bridge for softer shots and vice versa. You may consider limiting your longest bridge to 9-11". A final note: join Archer and Reyes in keeping your cue as level as possible on rail shots.

Warm Up Strokes

The proper use of warm up strokes is an integral part of a player's shooting routine. They are used to lock in your aim, build confidence, and to gain a feel for your stroke and the speed of the shot. There are a wide variety of warm up strokes patterns. Some very fine players, when in peak form, will land on the table, take 1-3 quick warm up strokes and fire away with uncanny accuracy.

In today's world of pool, however, the players who use a set pattern seem to consistently play the best pool. Their routines are very repetitious. The number of warm up strokes varies and is dependent on the difficulty of the shot. If you want to know how a player views the difficulty of a shot, count their warm up strokes and compare it to their average. That's just what I've done with Archer and Reyes. You will find great value in studying the results of their patterns, especially if you are unsure of your warm up stroke routine.

Archer

The chart below shows the distribution of warm up strokes for all non-break shots. Archer averaged

3.36 warm up strokes per shot. Archer precisely fits the number of warm up strokes to the shot, much more so than Reyes. Archer typically used 2-3 warm up strokes on routine shots. This enables him to conserve his energy. Archer will use 5-6 warm up strokes on tougher shots. On a demanding table length billiard, he used eight warm up strokes. In sum, Archer used 2-4 warm up strokes on 80% of his shots.

Archer varies the length of his warm up strokes to match the speed of the shot. He may only use a series of two to three inch warm up strokes on a soft shot, while on a power shot he may use a series of warm up strokes exceeding eight inches.

Warm Up Strokes

Number	Archer	Reyes
0	1	0
1	2	0
2	17	1
3	33	7
4	18	30
5	7	46
6	6	14
7	0	2
8	1	1
Total	**85**	**101**
Average	**3.36**	**4.74**

Reyes

Reyes used from two to eight warm up strokes. This average includes only his full warm up strokes. He also uses about 1-3 very short strokes during his warm up stroking routine.

Reyes warm up strokes tend to be quite long, but he will use shorter warm up strokes for softer shots.

Reyes' range was much tighter than Archer's, as he used from 4-6 warm up strokes on 89% of his shots. Reyes' high of eight warm up strokes came on a difficult side pocket cut shot that he barely missed. Reyes' tight pattern indicates that he is more of a rhythm player than Archer as he likes to stay closer to a preset pattern. Reyes is always in motion from the moment he begins to bend down until the completion of his follow through. As soon as his bridge is affixed to the table, he immediately starts warm up stroking.

Warm Up Strokes Fit the Shot

The table below shows how many warm up strokes were used by Archer and Reyes. The number used depends on the difficulty of the shot. The table shows these players use no set number of warm up strokes. Instead, the table demonstrates that your pattern should vary depending on your sense of the difficulty of the shot. The number of warm up strokes is not something you should be thinking about when playing a shot. Instead, the correct amount is determined automatically based on how you feel about the shot as you go about executing it.

of Warm Up Strokes Fits the Shot

	Archer	Reyes
Easy shots	1-2	2-3
Average shots	3-4	4-5
Tough shots	5-8	6-8

Your Game: Warm Up Strokes Fit Shot
I strongly advise that you do what the pros do: fit your number of warm up strokes to the shot. Don't start counting your warm up strokes when you're playing. Instead, enlist the aid of your instructor or a friend. Have them record your warm up strokes on a variety of shots. Then review the results. The idea is to discover your pattern and to see if it needs modification. Are you missing because you are shooting too quickly or are you endlessly sawing wood?

You should also adopt the habit of varying the length of you warm up strokes to more closely mirror the length of your final stroke.

Timing the Stroke
About the Study
I have wondered for some time how long the pool stroke takes, so I timed 121 shots from the match. The test covered 53 of Archer's shots and 68 shots for Reyes. These were all position play shots in which I got a reasonably good look at their stroke.

I used a VCR with excellent special effects, so I am reasonably confident of the accuracy of the timing for the backstroke and forward stroke.

There are no errors greater than 1/30 of a second on any shot. Furthermore, I feel there is enough data that any errors in either direction (too much or too little time) will largely cancel each other out.

Timing the pause if any, which comes at the transition point from backstroke to forward stroke, was tough due to camera angles and because it happens so quickly. My goal was to achieve an overall average that is representative of the player's style, recognizing that this is very difficult to measure without using high-speed photography.

My analysis of the pause was aided by simply observing their strokes in slow motion. This would amplify any time spent in the transition phase. Even with the tape running at only 10% of the speed with which the shots were played, there was little to no apparent pause by either player.

The 3 Phases of the Stroke

The Backstroke

Archer draws the cue back slowly, taking about as much time to complete the backstroke as Reyes even though he covers far less ground due to his use of shorter bridges.

Reyes swings into his final stroke at a rapid pace as indicated by the average time of his backstroke, which is about the same as Archers even though it covers a much greater distance.

The Pause

Archer pauses for an average of about a 1/30 of a second at the end of his backstroke, which seems well suited to his slow and deliberate style. Reyes keeps moving until the completion of his follow through with little if any pause at the point of transition. Because of this, it would take extremely high-speed photography to accurately measure the length of his pause, which I estimate at about 1/100 of a second.

Stroke Speed (average of all shots)
Stroke in Fractions of a Second

	Archer	Reyes
Backstroke	.317	.312
Pause	.033	.011
Fwd. Stroke	.189	.207
Total	.539	.530

The Forward Stroke

The forward stroke was timed from the moment the cue started forward until contact with the cue ball. The table above shows that Archer's average forward stroke took .189 seconds. Reyes' took nearly 10% longer at .207 seconds, partially because he uses longer bridges.

The table below shows the speeds used by each player during the forward stroke. Reyes' forward stroke takes longer to unfold than Archer's, as the cue must travel down a longer bridge.

The total time of the forward stroke does not indicate the speed at contact because the cue is accelerating. In addition, it is very difficult to measure wrist action and its affect on the speed of the stroke as it usually takes place a split second before contact.

Forward Stroke 1/30 Second

	Archer	Reyes
4/30	.170	.074
5/30	.283	.206
6/30	.302	.382
7/30	.226	.162
8/30	.000	.162
9/30	.019	.015

**Average Stroke Speed for All Shots
(except the Power Draw Shot)
In Fractions of a Second**

	Archer	Reyes
Backstroke	.319	.314
Pause	.033	.012
Fwd. Stroke	.196	.217
Total	.548	.543

Power Draw

For the purposes of this study I have defined a power draw shot as one that requires at least a medium hard stroke (6) (see PYBNB, page 138). The pace of a power draw stroke is very much the same on the back stroke as for other shots. However, it is quite different on the forward stroke.

I timed 10 power draw shots for Archer and 11 for Reyes. Archer's overall stroke is 9% faster for power draw shots than for all other shots. His forward stroke for power draw shots is about 25% faster. Reyes overall stroke is 17% faster for power draw shots while his forward stroke is a whopping 37% quicker than it is on average for all other shots.

The key to these players ability to draw the ball effectively is a smooth but rapid acceleration of the cue to and through the cue ball. While this comes as no big surprise, many players have a big problem executing this kind of stroke. Most errors are caused by tensing up the moment the forward stroke begins in an attempt to muscle the shot.

The 3 Phases of a Power Draw Shot
Stroke Speed in Fractions of a Second

	Archer	Reyes
Backstroke	.310	.300
Pause	.033	.006
Fwd. Stroke	.157	.158
Total	.500	.464

The Pace of the Stroke

The table below shows the range of times spent on the final backstroke, pause (if any) and forward stroke up to the point of contact.

Archer took between 16/30 and 18/30 of a second to complete 59% of his final strokes. Reyes, whose pace is slightly quicker, consumed between 15/30 and 17/30 of a second on 54% of his position plays. The remainder of each player's times were spread across the spectrum from 10-20 30ths of a second as shown.

Total Time of Shots % (1/30 second)

	Archer		Reyes	
Time	#	%	#	%
10	1	.015	0	.000
12	3	.057	3	.044
13	0	.000	4	.059
14	6	.113	10	.147
15	6	.113	12	.176
16	13	.245	14	.206
17	10	.189	11	.162
18	8	.151	8	.118
19	3	.057	5	.074
20	3	.057	1	.015
Total	**53**		**68**	

The wide range of times spent executing the stroke emphasizes the need for learning to vary the pace of your stroke to the particular shot at hand.

Soft Follow Shots

The majority of strokes that took .6 seconds or longer were used on soft easy follow shots. This indicates that these players took advantage of the relatively routine nature of these shots to use an unhurried stroke that enables them to really feel the speed of the shot.

Archer's Short Stroke

Archer employs a rather compact stroke for a good many of his shots. His elbow rises slightly on his backstroke and it drops after contact on the follow through of most shots.

On some soft shots, Archer's bridge often measures no more than five inches. It appears that his maximum stroke for power shots is around 9-10". Archer alters the length of his backstroke to meet the needs of the shot. On softer shots, he may take the cue back no more than two to four inches.

A short stroke like Archer's is good for accuracy, and it insures that you will accelerate through the shot. It may at times, however, have a slightly negative effect on your speed control.

Reyes' Rhythmic Action

Reyes is in constant motion from the time he begins to take his stance. Reyes' stroke features lots of motion, especially in elbow and upper arm. On his final stroke his elbow rises noticeably. He uses a fairly long bridge on most shots. And on most shots he will take the cue back all the way into his bridge loop. If he is using one of his patented extra long rail bridges, however, he will often take the cue back well short of his bridge hand. His forward stroke starts slowly, but accelerates sharply, especially on power shots. Reyes has one of the longest, straightest and most elegant follow throughs in the game.

Reyes sets up with the tip low. This technique allows him to get a better look at the cue ball prior to the final stroke. He must adjust his cue angle when going through the shot to strike the cue ball where intended. I feel that most amateurs would be better off placing the tip where they intend to strike the cue ball. I wouldn't recommend this technique unless you've been using it for several years with good results.

Your Game: A Smooth Backstroke

Archer and Reyes demonstrated the value of a smooth, tension free backstroke. Each paused for no more than a split second (1/30 of a second or less) at the end of their backstroke, yet this was long enough to produce a smooth transition.

If you have trouble with the transition, try starting your final stroke at the same pace as you use on your warm up strokes. **Let the acceleration build gradually, with the pace really picking up in the second half of the forward stroke.**

If the suggestion above is not effective at smoothing your transition, consider a slightly longer pause. Top pros Buddy Hall and Allison Fisher both use a pronounced pause at the end of their backstroke with great results.

Use a Short Stroke

A short stroke can increase your accuracy on a long shot when power is not a main requirement of the shot. It can also help you to match the length of your stroke to softer shots. By using a shorter stroke on soft shots, you can avoid the tendency to decelerate through the shot.

The Value of Rhythm

Reyes is a prime example of the value of staying in motion during the execution phase of the shot cycle. His rhythmic aproach provides a platform for consistancy at the highest level of performance.

Additional Information

See Chapters 1 and 2 of *Play Your Best Pool* and pages 1-7 of *Play Your Best Nine Ball*.

The Spectrum of Speed

Introduction

In this section are findings on each player's speeds of stroke. Speed of stroke was derived in most cases by measuring the cue ball's speed from contact with the tip to contact with the object ball. When it was not possible to get an accurate measurement, I viewed the shot several times and made a judgment call. After watching countless shots over the last 32 years, it is not difficult to estimate the speed of stroke. For example, I can tell the difference between a medium stroke and a medium hard stroke with a good degree of accuracy. All speeds refer to the Spectrum of Speed, which measures speeds on a scale of 1-10.

Position Across the Spectrum

The 1-10 scale defines the boundaries of the Spectrum of Speed. The table shows the results from 131 position plays.

Nearly 80% of all position plays fall in the range of soft to medium hard. The 3-6MPH zone is one that promotes accuracy and excellent speed control. One reason why many of the pros shots fell into this range is they are experts at using angles to play position. They avoid the long small angle shots in which the cue ball must be sent a considerable distance to the position zone. For more on proper angles, see pages 140-142, **PYBNB**).

Spectrum of Speeds   **Use of Speeds**

Position Plays
The Spectrum of Speed

Speed	MPH	PP	%
1 Extremely Soft	1.5	0	0.0
2 Very Soft	2.0	10	7.6
3 Soft	3.0	20	15.3
4 Medium Soft	4.0	30	22.9
5 Medium	5.0	26	19.8
6 Medium Hard	6.0	27	20.6
7 Hard	7.0	8	6.1
8 Very Hard	8.0	6	4.6
9 Extremely Hard	10.0	4	3.1
Total		**131**	

The scarcity of shots played with a very soft stroke underscores the player's dislike of shooting position plays with a very soft stroke except at very short range. Shooting very easy is great for speed control, but can lead to missed shots, especially under pressure.

Runouts Across the Spectrum

There were 17 gamewinning runouts in the match. Four of these runouts required at least five different speeds of stroke (not counting the 9-ball). They are listed below. Included is Reyes masterful runout in Game 16, in which he used six different speeds on six consecutive shots! His speeds were: 7, 8, 3, 9, 5, 6.

Games with 5 or More Speeds:
4, 6, 13, 16

Power Shots: Speed 7 and Above

There were 18 position plays on which Archer and Reyes used a speed of 7 (hard) or above. The players were successful on 14 of these shots, which is a pretty good batting average. There was only one missed ball among the four unsuccessful shots, which underscores these pros amazing accuracy. The three other mistakes were due to errors on difficult position plays.

How Power Shots Originate

There were three reasons why a pro would wind up having to use speed 7 or above: 1) It's the first shot, so they have no choice; 2) they commit a positional error; 3) the layout almost certainly dictates that they will have to use a hard stroke during their run. The 18 shots are summarized below. The list also shows four turn ending mistakes. Two resulted from difficult first shots and two others came from positional errors.

9 First shots. Errors: 2
5 Positional mistakes. Errors: 2
4 Layout dictates a hard stroke. Errors: 0

We can conclude from this table that: 1) the pros are skillful at gaining control of the table with a difficult first shot; 2) a sure way to lose the table is from a positional error; 3) the pros excel at playing layouts that include a shot which requires a hard stroke.

Learning from the Power Shots

The 18 position plays where the players used a stroke speed of 7H (hard) or greater are listed below. You will notice that there is a good mixture of draw, follow, stun and draw/stun shots.

These shots are worthy of further study. Observe carefully how Archer and Reyes deliver a smooth and authoritative stroke on the vast majority of these challenging shots.

Power Shots	Speed	Shot #
Game 2 - Page 8		
7-ball C 1-rail draw	**7H**	2-7
Game 4 - Page 16		
7-ball A 3-rail draw	**9EH**	4-10
Game 5 - Page 17		
2-ball A 1-rail follow.	**8VH**	5-1
Game 6 - Page 26		
8-ball B 1 rail draw.	**7H**	6-8
Game 8 - Page 28		
1-ball A 2-rails follow.	**7H**	8-3

Speed on Safeties and Kick Shots

The speed used on safeties and kick shots is presented on one table so you can easily see the difference in how each category of shots is played. The vast majority of safeties are played with a speed of 4 (medium soft) or below. This shows the value of a soft stroke in maximizing cue ball control.

A medium hard stroke {6} or faster was used on 11 of 15 kick shots. The wide variety of speeds shows that the pros play strategic kick shots and that they really fit the speed of stroke to the shot.

Many amateurs, on the other hand, use a hard stroke on most kick shots with the goals of maybe getting a hit and a fortunate roll.

The Spectrum of Speed

Speed	Safeties	Kicks
1 Extremely Soft	1	0
2 Very Soft	6	1
3 Soft	5	0
4 Medium Soft	3	3
5 Medium	1	0
6 Medium Hard	1	2
7 Hard	0	4
8 Very Hard	0	2
9 Extremely Hard	0	3
10 The Break 15.0+		
Total	**17**	**15**

The 9-Ball

There is no need to play position when shooting the 9-ball. Therefore, the players generally choose the speed of stroke that maximized their chances of pocketing the 9-ball. The table shows they only used speeds 3-7 when playing the 9-ball. Furthermore, all but one shot on the 9-ball was played between soft and medium hard.

The Spectrum of Speed on 9-Balls

Speed	#
3 Soft	6
4 Medium Soft	2
5 Medium	4
6 Medium Hard	4
7 Hard	1

The vast majority of their shots on the 9-ball were at small angles from relatively close range. The player's main objective on the last shot was to pocket the 9-ball. Nevertheless, when they were faced with a cut angle of more than a few degrees, they would make sure to send the cue ball down a path after contact that virtually eliminated any chance of a scratch.

Summary of Speeds of Stroke

The table below gives you the average speed of stroke for all of the primary categories of shots, excluding the break shot. The "average shot", interestingly enough, clocked in at just under medium at 4.8MPH.

	App. Ave. Speed	**Spectrum**
Safeties	3.03 MPH	3S
9-Ball	4.53 MPH	4MS-5M
Position Plays	4.85 MPH	5M
Kick Shots:	6.67 MPH	7H
All Shots	4.80 MPH	5M

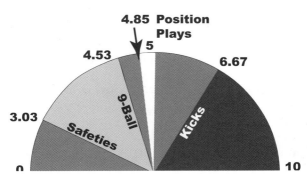

Your Game: Mastering Speed Control

Archer and Reyes are like concert pianists who roam far and wide up and down the keyboard. Each has demonstrated mastery using speeds from 1 to 9. Their ability comes from years of play during which they both developed a keen awareness for the ideal speed for every type of shot.

You can start to develop speed control by paying close attention to the ending location of your shots. Did the cue ball stop on the target or come up short or long on a particular type of shot? You need to store these pieces of information in your memory bank so you employ the correct speed when that type of shot comes up again. Your patience and attention to your results will be rewarded over time with an increasingly fine sense of touch.

Your ultimate goal is to master the entire Spectrum of Speeds. You may, however, get your best results by first mastering shots in the 3-6 range. Once you have developed the ability to stop the cue ball near your target on these shots, then proceed to the shots at both ends of the spectrum.

There are also a number of drills in Chapter 15 of **PYBNB** that can be useful in developing your sense of touch.

Shotmaking

There were very few missed shots in the match as you might suspect in a contest featuring the worlds two top ranked players. Archer, who faced fewer tough shots than Reyes, nevertheless shot with amazing accuracy, missing just one tough shot in Game 16. Reyes was equally accurate on routine shots. His five misses came on a variety of challenging shots as listed below.

The tables below list both the great shots and the misses. Reyes made several more great shots than Archer but lost the contest. This was in part due to the fact he also missed many more shots than Archer.

Great Shots

Game 1 #1 Archer 1-ball   **Shot #1-1**
This position play required Archer to send the cue ball across the table twice and between the 3 and 7-balls while avoiding a scratch.

Game 4 #2 Reyes 7-ball   **Shot #4-10**
Hitting this massive draw shot accurately with an extremely hard stroke was a major challenge.

Game 6 #2 Reyes 1-ball   **Shot #6-1**
Reyes played pinpoint shape through traffic.

Game 8 #3 Reyes 1-ball   **Shot #8-3**
Reyes fanned in a table length 75-degree cut and got shape on the 2-ball.

Game 9 #3 Archer 9-ball Billiard Shot #9-3
Archer made the 1-ball and then the 9-ball on a table length stun billiard.

Game 10 #2 Reyes 3-ball   **Shot #10-3**
This shot vividly showcased Reyes' technique on a long draw shot.

#4 Reyes 6-ball   **Shot #10-8**
Reyes had the choice of playing safe or going for the bank. He pounded home the bank and ran out.

Game 14 #3 Reyes 2-ball   Shot #14-3
Reyes deftly executed a 3-rail route through traffic on the first ball.

Game 16 #4 Reyes 3-ball   Shot #16-6
This shot required an accurate and powerful stroke (speed) and the proper cueing.

6-ball   Shot # 16-8   This was a two rail cross table power follow shot off the rail with inside english. GREAT!!

Game 19 #6 Reyes 4-ball   Shot #19-9
The cue ball's direction was expertly controlled with stun/draw.

Game 20 #2 Archer 1-ball   Shot #20-1
An excellent long shot considering that survival in the match and the tournament was on the line.

Missed Shots

Game 4   Shot #4-4
Reyes misses a two-way. Probably equal parts shot and safety. The ball barely missed, which indicated that Reyes was making an all effort to pocket the ball.

Game 8   Shot #8-4
Reyes miscued on a draw shot. He was trying to accomplish two objectives, which may have affected his concentration. I don't think I've ever seen him miscue on any other shot.

Game 15 Shot #20-1
Reyes missed on a 4-rail position play.
This shot required a very hard stroke while bridging on the rail, which certainly makes this an excusable error.

Game 16   Shot #16-4
Archer barely missed a long and difficult shot off the end rail.

Game 19   Shot #19-1
Reyes missed a long rail bank shot. This miss might be more about poor shot selection than anything else.

Game 21   Shot #21-5
Reyes missed a moderately difficult cut shot. This is Reyes' one unforgivable miss as it came on a shot you would expect Reyes to make at a crucial stage of the match. I estimate Reyes would make this about 90% of the time or more.

Shotmaking Summary

	Attempts	Made	%
Archer	58	57	.983
Reyes	74	69	.932
Overall	132	126	.955

Your Game: Don't Miss (Very Often)
The very top pros almost never miss routine shots. They only miss difficult shots infrequently and by the smallest of margins. So if you want to be a top player the message is clear: don't miss routine shots, and seldom miss the tougher ones either.

The one sure way to limit your misses is to become a superb shotmaker, especially under pressure. There's certainly no big mystery about that. You can improve your shotmaking with practice and work on your fundamentals. Pay close attention to your misses so you can learn to hone in on the pocket. For example, if you overcut a certain shot consistently, you should note that tendency and make the necessary adjustment.

You can also cut down on missed shots simply by gaining a better understanding of your capabilities. This will help you to decide which shots to go for, and which to pass in favor of a safety.

The Break

Archer's Technique

Archer is very methodical about the break shot. He will check the cue ball and clean it if necessary. In addition, he regularly conducts rack inspections. It appears as if he places much more emphasis on the break than Reyes, who seems to take a far more casual approach to the break shot.

Archer changed break positions four times during the match, including Game 18, in which he broke and ran out to tie the match. Before breaking on the double hill game, Archer spent a long time deciding where to position the cue ball.

Archer will often assume his break stance, then get up to check his grip before resuming his routine. Archer used an average of nine warm up strokes for the break, or nearly 3x his average of 3.36 on non-break shots. On the double hill break, Archer used 13 warm up strokes, even though he averaged only 8.6 on the previous 10 breaks. This shows how he gears up for a major effort on the most important shot in pro Nine Ball.

Archer cues low at address with his backhand higher than it will be at contact. The lowering of the arm on the forward swing raises the tip to near dead center contact with the cue ball.

In slow motion you will see lots of body movement during Archers warm up strokes, especially on the last one, as he is gearing up to explode into the cue ball.

Reyes' Technique

Reyes used more warm up strokes than Archer on non-break shots, but far less on the break shot. His average of six warm up strokes was only 1.25 more than he uses on non-break shots. This shows that Reyes really sticks to his rhythm on all shots including the break.

During this match, the break seemed to be just another shot to Reyes, but with a somewhat harder stroke than he uses for position plays requiring a hard stroke.

Warm Up Strokes / Break Shot

#	Archer	Reyes
5		2
6		6
7	3	2
8	1	
9	4	
10	1	
11	1	
13	1	
Aver.	9.0	6.0

Summary of Archer's Break

Archer's break was ineffective throughout most of the match, but he did manage to win three times in his first inning. In addition, he was able to break and run the 18th game to tie the match. He was also able to make a ball on the break on the double hill game, which enabled him to gain control of the table.

Summary of Reyes' Break

Reyes soft break was highly effective at making balls. Even so, Reyes was only able to post a 4-6 record on his break. This indicates he didn't take full advantage of his break.

Archer was much more effective than Reyes when he made a ball on the break, winning four of four games. If his break had been working, he may have won by a much larger margin. There were no scratches, which was attributable mostly to skill, since both players hit the 1-ball very accurately and, to a lesser degree, to luck, which is always a factor on the break.

Break Summary

	Archer	Reyes
Breaks	11	10
W/L on Break	5-6	4-6
Total Balls Made	6	11
Breaks-Ball Made	4	7
Break and Run	2	1
9-ball on Break	1	1
Give up second player run	3	1

Combined Total

17 balls Pocketed in 21 games.
.81 balls per break.
Breaker won only 9 of 21 games.

Break Position

Reyes made a ball in four of five breaks from Position A through Game 8 while Archer was one for three from that location. Starting in Game 9 Archer changed break positions four times in the next five games, perhaps feeling a bit of frustration from coming up empty repeatedly. Meanwhile the announcers suggested that he consider copying Reyes softer break, which was working quite well.

Balls on the Break

Position	Archer	Reyes
A	4 in 5 Br.	11 in 10 Br.
B	0 in 1 Br.	-
C	2 in 4 Br.	-
Total	**6 in 11 Br.**	**11 in 10 Br.**

The above table shows that Position A was the most productive spot.

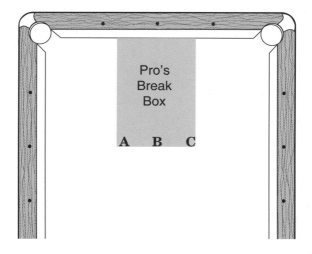

Break Speed

Reyes' kick shot in Game 10 clocked in at 12.6 MPH. This was the hardest struck non-break shot in the match. In comparison, Reyes break speed was about 22MPH according to my estimates. This gap between the hardest hit non-break shot and the break shows the power break is not remotely like any other shot in pool.

Timing the break was difficult at best. The cue ball took a little less than 4/30 of a second to reach the rack on Reyes break, which equals about 22MPH. When Archer broke, the cue ball needed a little over 3/30 of second to reach the 1-ball, which translates to about 26MPH. This reading is in line with the break speed Archer recorded at a contest held by *Pool & Billiard Magazine* a month later at the BCA Trade Show.

Your Game: Seek Power and Accuracy
This match demonstrated the virtues of hitting the 1-ball accurately as neither player scratched on the break. Your number one lesson, therefore, is to start paying strict attention to the cue ball's path after contact with the 1-ball. It is your surest indicator of a solid break.

The power break requires a separate set of mechanics. The most precise element, as shown by both players, is the raising of the body and dropping of the shooting arm on the final stroke. The higher body position is necessary to clear the way for a powerful arm swing to and through the cue ball.

When your break is failing to make balls even though you are striking the 1-ball solidly, consider moving to another spot and/or changing speeds. Also play attention to your opponent's break. Consider copying it, especially if it is producing good results.

Additional Information: See Chapter 2 in **PYBNB**.

Position Play
Number of Rails in Position Play

The table below summarizes the number or rails each player used in playing position. One rail shape was the most common by far. Archer used it on nearly half of his position plays while Reyes used a single cushion on nearly 58% of his position plays.

Position plays that used no-rail and two-rail routes were next in importance. Even though Nine Ball requires you to often send the cue ball long distances relative to other pool games, three-rail routes were only used on about 6% of all position plays.

Position Plays

Rails	Archer	%	Reyes	%
0	13	22.8	12	17.4
1	28	49.1	40	57.8
2	13	22.8	12	17.4
3	3	5.6	5	7.3
Total	**57**		**69**	

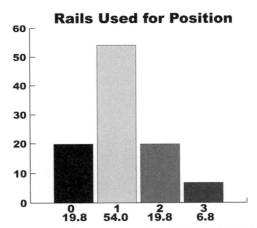

Rails Used for Position

| 0
19.8 | 1
54.0 | 2
19.8 | 3
6.8 |

Your Game: Master 1-Rail Position

Nine Ball, as you've no doubt been counseled, is largely about leaving yourself with the proper angle. The correct angle allows you to send the cue ball where needed without having to continuously resort to power shots.

After playing most cut shots, the cue ball is going to naturally strike at least one rail. It follows that mastering cue ball direction off the first rail is a foundation to solid position play.

ABC's of Position Play

I use a three letter system for grading the difficulty of position plays. My somewhat subjective rating is based on the difficulty of pocketing the shot and on getting good position on the next ball. C's are very routine shots. The pros executed the C's with great precision as there was only one error on a C in the entire match, which came in Game 10. The remaining errors occurred mostly on A's. The number of C's and B's added up to 88.9% of all position plays! One of the reasons for a disproportionately high percentage of C's and B's is that the pros play such great position and patterns. They are experts, for example, at not turning a potential C into an A because of a positional error. In contrast, amateurs constantly face A's because of missed position.

Rts.	Archer	%	Reyes	%	Total	%
C	31	54.4	38	55.1	69	54.8
B	24	42.1	21	31.0	45	36.1
A	2	3.5	10	14.5	12	11.1

Your Game: Routine Racks Made Easy
The key to the pros ability to run out lies largely in not turning easy runouts into wild adventures. If you can master the C and B position routes, you will be able to consistently run out the routine racks. In addition, you will be on your way to running more complex layouts at least a fair percentage of the time.

Additional information: On pages 70-106 of PYBNB are a wide variety of position routes rated C and B. I suggest that you systematically work your way through these routes until you've got them all mastered, for they are the building blocks for running out easily and effortlessly.

The Primary Emphasis of Position

In the introduction there is an explanation of the primary emphasis on position play and the notation that shows it throughout the book. When rating a shot, I tried to view the difficulty of pocketing the shot from the perspective of both a pro and amateur. If I hadn't done this, the emphasis on pocketing would have been considerably less since the pros are such tremendous shotmakers.

The list below is your handy reference to shots that can teach you how to recognize the primary emphasis in a wide variety of position plays.

Your Game: Two Things at Once
The old joke about being able to walk and chew gum is really the essence of playing position. To excel at position play, you have to make the ball and control the cue ball. The difficulty of this task on any shot is related to your skill and to the challenge of the shot. The key is to recognize what needs to be emphasized on a shot and to put your attention on performing that element as well as possible.

As your skills increase in the three possible areas of primary emphasis (pocketing, direction, speed) this has the effect of allowing you to really focus on the most important element of a shot. For

example, Archer or Reyes may be able to really
zero in on directional control while giving much
less concern to pocketing the shot. In the same situation, an amateur may be so concerned with just
making the ball that their directional control suffers. In other word, success begets success.

Additional Information: For more information
on the Primary Emphasis, see page 65, **PYBNB**.

Runouts
Runout Opportunities

Archer converted 89% of his runout attempts. His
only failure came from a pocketing error in Game
19. Meanwhile, Reyes was successful on only 69%
of his attempts largely because he was confronted
with a series of difficult key shots. Reyes got
hooked on an easy position play in Game 10, but
still won. His other failures came from missing two
difficult shots and from corner hooking himself.

Archer's eight gamewinning runouts averaged
7.13 balls while Reyes' nine winning runouts averaged 7.22 balls. These figures attest to these great
players talents at shotmaking, pattern recogni-
tion, and position play.

Run Out Conversion Percentage

	Possible	Conver.	%	Ave. Balls
Archer	9	8	88.9	7.13
Reyes	13	9	69.2	7.22
Total	22	17	77.3	7.18

Run Out Successes & Failures

Below is a listing of both players' runout attempts. When their name is underlined it indicates they did not complete the runout. When their name is italicized, it indicates that they won by means other than a runout. My **ABC** system for rating the difficulty of a layout is explained in the introduction. The rating of the layouts difficulty is shown last.

1 **Archer** RO - 7 balls. **B**

2 **Reyes** RO - 9 balls. **C**

3 **Reyes** RO - 8 balls. **C**

4 **Archer** missed shape on rack that's probably not runnable.
 Reyes RO - 7 balls. **B**

5 <u>Reyes</u> corner hooked himself on tough table length position play.
 Archer RO - 6 balls. **C**

6 *Reyes* RO - 9 balls. **B+**

7 **Reyes** made the 9-ball on the break.

8 **Reyes** miscued, tough to run out, no failure.
 Archer made easy 2 shot RO.

9 *Archer* made a billiard on the 9-ball.

10 <u>Reyes</u> hooked himself on a routine shot.
 Archer played a poor safety.
 Reyes RO - 4 balls. **B**

11 **Reyes** lost position, played a poor safety. Too tough to call a RO failure.
 Archer RO - 4 balls. **C+**

12 *Archer* made the 9-ball on the break.

13 **Reyes** RO - 9-balls. **C+**

14 **Reyes** RO - 7 balls. **B+**

15 <u>Reyes</u> missed a tough 4-rail position shot.
 Archer RO - 8 balls. **C+**

16 **Reyes** missed shape, too tough to run.
Archer missed a tough shot, too tough to call
a RO failure.
Reyes RO - 7 balls. **A**

17 **Archer** RO - 9-balls. **B**

18 **Archer** RO - 8 balls. **A**

19 <u>Archer</u> Hooked himself on a routine shot.
Reyes RO - 5 balls. **A**

20 **Archer** RO - 9 balls. B

21 Archer lost the cue ball on combo, not a
legitimate RO.
Reyes missed a run out opportunity on a
medium difficult shot.
Archer RO - 6 balls. **C**

The table below summarizes the difficulty of the
gamewinning layouts each player faced. Reyes was
confronted with several more difficult racks than
Archer.

Run Out Rating Summary

Rating	Archer	Reyes
C	2	2
C+	2	1
B	3	2
B+	0	2
A	1	2

Your Game: **Up Your Conversion Rate**
The discussion above certainly underscores the
pros skill at consistently running out from long
range. This leads to the question: are you aware of
your conversion percentage? Are you at the stage
where you run out infrequently or not at all after

the break? Do you know where your run outs typically begin? Knowing your run out distance tells you where you stand in the world of competitive Nine Ball. This is vital in choosing which events to play in and for handicapping.

In addition, your run out distance can also help you in plotting strategy. For example, if you typically run no more than 4-5 balls, you might wish to take well calculated shots at the money balls early in a game. Finally, by facing your current runout range, you have established an important benchmark, which can spur you to further developing your game.

Ball-In-Hand

Archer committed just one foul, which came in Game 4. Reyes committed six fouls, which is an astonishing figure when you consider Reyes is a master at defensive play and is a wizard in the kicking game. It should be noted that one foul was intentional and at least two of his fouls were the result of bad luck on well-executed kick shots.

The first foul led to a loss in five of six games. This shows how devastating scratches are at the pro level. The fouls and game in which they took place are listed below.

4 Archer missed a hit on a kick shot.   **#4-6**
   Reyes ran out.

5 Reyes took an intentional foul.   **#5-4**
   Archer played shape for a safety.
   Reyes scratched on a kick shot.   **#5-7**
   Archer ran out.

8 Reyes miscued, knocking the cue ball off the
     table.   **#8-5**
     Archer pocketed an easy combo on the 9-ball.

15 Reyes missed a tough shot and scratched.
     Archer ran out.   **#15-2**

17 Reyes played a superb kick but scratched.
     Archer ran out.   **#17-3**

19 Reyes played a poor kick and scratched.
                          #19-4
     Archer failed to run out.

Your Game: Study Your Fouls

Most amateurs have a tendency to head for the chair with a scowl on their face after fouling. Rather than bemoaning your fate, take a couple of moments to analyze how each foul happened. Study each of your fouls so that type of foul is less likely to happen again. Then start to prepare mentally for your next turn. When you are not competing but are watching others play, observe their fouls and learn from someone else's mistakes.

In the amateur game, I constantly see far too many fouls that are committed for all of the wrong reasons. The leading causes of unnecessary fouls are:

• Slamming the cue ball off the table on the break.
• Scratching repeatedly in the same pocket on the break.
• Playing "give up" kick shots.
• Not knowing the cue balls path after contact with the object ball.

If you discover you are guilty of any of these infractions, you have an area of your game that is ripe for immediate improvement.

Push Outs

The pros hate to give their opponent any kind of chance to play a shot or safety. This is evidenced by the fact there was only one push out in the entire match. In amateur play, a pushout might have also been used in Game 19.

Game 9

Reyes pushed out. Archer let Reyes have the shot. Reyes played safe and left Archer a long and difficult billiard on the 9-ball, which Archer pocketed.

Your Game: A Strategic Weapon

The push out is viewed as a tactic of last resort by the pros as they hate to let their opponent to the table. In the amateur game, however, the push out is more widely used and is a valuable tactical weapon. This is especially true if you have skills your opponent doesn't, or if you are the more knowledgeable player. You can use safeties as a means of bluffing your opponent into taking a shot when there is nothing there. Your opponent may also let you shoot after a push because they don't see the safety you have planned.

Addition Information: See Chapter 10, **PYBNB.**

The safety play was wildly erratic in this match. There were only four safeties that lead directly to a win, and four that lead immediately to a loss. The remaining 11 safeties were part of defensive battles, including five in the final game.

Archer hooked Reyes on six of 12 safeties while Reyes hooked Archer on only two of seven safeties. There were at least six times they failed to hook the other even though a snooker was quite possible. This is one of the most surprising stats of all, considering each player's expert cue ball control.

Shot 4-2
#2 Archer left Reyes a shot. Safety loses.

Shot 5-2
#1 Reyes' masse safety attempt left Archer with an easy return safety.

Shot 5-3
#2 Archer's safety hooked Reyes.

Shot 5-6
#4 Archer's safety hooked Reyes.

Shot 5-8
#6 Archer's safety hooked Reyes. Safety wins.

Shot 8-1
#1 Reyes' safe gave Archer a safety opportunity.

Shot 8-2
#2 Archer's safety left Reyes a long cut.

Shot 9-2
#2 Reyes left Archer with a long shot. Safety loses.

Shot 10-7
#3 Archer's left Reyes a run out. Safety loses.

Shot 11-4

#1 **Reyes** safety left Archer with a shot. Safety loses.   **#11-4**

Shot 14-1

#1 **Reyes** played a two-way safety/shot and hooked Archer. **Safety** wins.

Shot 16-3

#2 **Reyes'** gave Archer a long shot. **Safety** wins.

Shot 17-1

#2 **Archer** hooked Reyes. **Safety** wins.

Shot 19-2

#3 **Archer** hooked Reyes. Reyes won when Archer failed to run out.

Shot 21-2

#1 **Archer** played safe (or missed a tough side pocket shot), hooking Reyes.

Shot 21-4

#3 **Archer's** safety left Reyes a tough shot.

Shot 21-6

#5 **Archer's** left Reyes a long shot or safety.

Shot 21-7

#6 **Reyes'** safety hooked Archer.

Shot 21-11

#9 **Archer's** safety hooked Reyes.

Summary of Safeties

	Win	Lose	Other	Total	Hooked
Archer	2	2	8	12	6
Reyes	2	2	3	7	2
Total	**4**	**4**	**11**	**19**	**8**

Your Game: Do What Others Won't

One of the surest roads to success in any endeavor is to do what others won't. When it comes to safety play, than means spending time practicing safeties. If you can consistently send the cue ball behind a blocker, you will dramatically increase you share of ball-in-hands and, in the process, greatly frustrate your opponents.

Additional Information: See Chapter 11 and pages 424-427 of PYBNB.

Kick Shots

Archer made contact on five of six kick shots while Reyes hit the object ball on all nine of his kick shots. Reyes scratched three times, losing two games. The most vital stat reveals that the players hit and then hooked their opponent on four of the 14 kick shots, a 29% average. That percentage warrants giving kick shots the extra effort these shots require (more on this in a later section). The kicker left his opponent a runout opportunity 47% of the time.

Shot 4-5
Archer kicked 1 rail and missed. Kick loses.
Shot 5-7
Reyes left Archer to an easy safety.
Shot 5-9
Reyes scratched on a kick shot. Kick loses.
Shot 10-6
Reyes kicked 1-rail and hit, but left Archer with a safety opportunity.

Shot 14-2
Archer's 1-rail kick left a shot. Kick loses.
Shot 17-2
Reyes kicked and hit the 1-ball but scratched. Kick loses.
Shot 19-3
Reyes 1-rail kick hit the 1-ball, but scratched.
Shot 19-8
Archer kicked 3-rails and hit the 5-ball, leaving a tough shot. Kick loses.
Shot 21-3
Reyes kicked 1 rail and hit, leaving the edge.
Shot 21-8
Archer kicked 3-rails, hit and hooked Reyes.
Shot 21-9
Reyes kicked 1-rail and left Archer hooked.
Shot 21-10
Archer kicked 1-rail into a long rail bank and made the 2-ball!
Shot 21-12
Reyes kicked 2-rails and hit, leaving a hook.
Shot 21-13
Archer kicked and hooked Reyes.
Shot 21-14
Reyes 3-rail kick and hit missed pocketing the 3-ball by an inch. **Kick** loses.

Kicking Summary

Player	#	Hit	Foul	Leaves Safe	Leaves Safe Op.	Leaves R.O. Op.
Reyes	9	9	3	2	3	4
Archer	6	5	1	3	0	3

Kick Shot Contact

Results of Kick Shots

Your Game: Rule #1: Make Contact
On all but the easiest kick shots your results are somewhat to highly unpredictable. But that should not stop you from giving each and every kick shot your best effort. As your skills improve, you will begin to see and execute strategic kick shots. But never lose sight of the golden rule of kicking: you've got to hit the ball to have even the slightest chance for something good to happen.
Additional Information: See Chapter 12 of PYBNB.

Match Time Statistics

Time is very revealing. It can show how the pros rate the difficulty or complexity of a shot. Their use of time also reveals mistakes and human tendencies that all pool players are subject to. Their usage of time shows the flow of their game. And time usage can also pinpoint the effects of pressure.

The pros generally play quickly, making very efficient use of their time. Their knowledge of the game, confidence, and superior shotmaking all work together to keep playing time to a minimum on most shots.

When top pros are confronted with a troublesome pattern, safety, or kick shot, they will take the necessary time to explore their options. Additional time is also spent in the execution phase of tough shots as they gear up for a superlative effort. This could include trying several bridges. They might also get back up off the shot if they don't feel comfortable or totally confident with their selection. And, as we discovered earlier, they will add extra warm up strokes to their routine on difficult shots.

Pros Versus Amateurs

When studying the sections below, keep in mind that these player's minds have been programmed to play pool. Their knowledge of the game allows them to quickly and efficiently read the table, consider the range of choices, and make the best decision, all things considered.

The pros knowledge, ironically, causes them to use more time in certain situations than an amateur would as they consider the options or hidden dangers in a position. Amateur players, while exploring the same layout, may use more or less time. For example, an amateur may shoot quickly on what only appears to be a routine position play because they don't see the dangers that need to be considered. Conversely, an amateur may require extra time to decipher a complex pattern because they lack the pros skill at reading the table.

Match Time

The entire match took over 1:42. If you exclude Game 21, which was a 21 minute marathon (including the time for racking), then the average game took only a little more than 4 minutes.

Match Summary

Total time:	1:42:08
Lag	00:11
Racking	17:30
Playing	85:25
Time per game	4:52
Games per hour	12.33
"Typical game"*	4.05*

* Excludes game 21, which took 20:36.

Time: Preparation and Execution

In the sections below I have broken the time spent on each shot into two categories: preparation and execution. Preparation begins the moment a player arrives at the table following the other player's turn, or when they finish the previous shot. Preparation ends the second the player assumes their final stance.

During the preparation phase the player does things like: surveying the table, decision making, and walking to the shot. The execution phase starts when the player assumes their stance and ends when their follow through is complete. I used increments of one second, so there will be small inaccuracies on certain shots. Any errors should largely cancel each other out due to the fairly large size of the sample on position plays.

Small mistakes in timing are even less critical on the shots that require a lot of planning time. The main objective is to identify trends and aberrations from the norm. The one second interval is more than sufficient to accomplish this goal.

Time in the Execution Phase

Once the players are down over a shot they have switched gears from thinking to executing, Their relatively short time spent executing each shot means that they stick to their routine, and are 100% in the execution mode while down over the ball. There were only 14 of 186 shots in which they took seven or more seconds to execute the shot. The 14 shots in which the players spent seven or more seconds are noted in the text with an **ET:7, ET:8,** or **ET:9.**

Time Spent in the Execution Phase

2-6 Seconds	172
7 Seconds	10
8 Seconds	3
9 Seconds	1

Gamewinning Run Outs

The match featured a number of lengthy gamewinning runouts. I was able to gather enough data to do an accurate sampling of each player's usage of time during a runout. The table shows that Archer used an average of over four seconds more than Reyes (13.84 vs. 9.75) moving to and preparing for the next shot. But once over the shot, Archer spent nearly a second less than Reyes. The longer time in the planning phase shows Archer's meticulous style. This is especially true when you consider that he, for the most part, faced easier layouts than Reyes.

Reyes moves rapidly and rhythmically around the table. He makes decisions rather quickly. However, he spends a good portion of his time in the execution phase of the shot cycle. Reyes follows a disciplined shooting routine that takes nearly a full second longer than Archer's. Reyes uses an average of almost 1.5 more warm up strokes per shot than Archer.

Effect of Pressure

Many players tend to slow their pace when under extreme pressure. The pros are often no exception. In the final game, Archer took an average of 23 seconds preparing for each shot in a routine run compared to his average of only 12.8 seconds on all other gamewinning runouts.

Time Spent Running Out (seconds/shot)

	Archer	Reyes	Combined
Preparation	13.84	9.75	11.66
Execution	4.05	4.88	4.49
Total	**17.89**	**14.63**	**16.16**

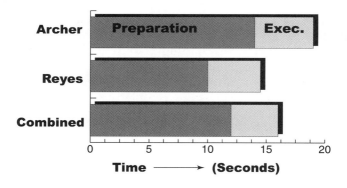

Preparing for Certain Types of Shots

The first shot of a gamewinning runout takes about six seconds more than average. Extra time is used to: plan a pattern, make a difficult shot to get in line, or for placing the cue ball with ball-in-hand. The key shot is often the first shot, but it can also occur later in the rack. Archer spent an average of 25.5 seconds planning the key shot while Reyes spent only 17.56 seconds. The 9-ball took an average of only 6.24 seconds of preparation. It is an extremely routine shot for the pros thanks to their superb position play.

Preparation Time for Certain Shots of Gamewinning Run Outs

	First Shot	**Longest**	**9-ball**	**Ave.**
Archer	17.88	25.50	6.63	13.84
Reyes	12.89	17.56	5.89	9.75
Average	**15.24**	**21.29**	**6.24**	**11.66**

Time Spent on A's versus C's

My **ABC** system for evaluating the difficulty of a rack coincided well with each player's use of time. As an example, Archer spent an average of only 10.67 seconds per shot in running Game 5, which was a C rated layout. In contrast, he spent 27.38 seconds per shot running Game 18, an A rated rack. Reyes consumed only 12.75 seconds per shot in Game 5 to run a C rated layout. He took 17.00 seconds per shot while completing the A rated Game 16.

Safeties

There were only 20 safeties and 15 kick shots, so the results in the next two sections are not a definitive sample. Still, the difference in time on these shots compared to runouts is large enough to draw some valid conclusions. The time spent on safeties was much greater than on position plays. It takes time to sift through the various options. Archer and Reyes both consumed close to 33 seconds planning and executing safeties. In contrast, their preparation time was about 12 seconds for the typical position play.

Time on Safeties

	Archer (12)	Reyes (8)	Combined
Planning	28.00	28.00	28.00
Executing	4.92	4.75	4.85
Total	**32.92**	**32.75**	**32.85**

Kick Shots

The planning phase for kick shots took an average of 44.6 seconds, which was substantially higher than that spent on safeties. This extra time was for: planning a strategic objective for the shot, choosing the route to the ball, deciding which part of the ball to contact, and deciding on the correct cueing and speed.

Time on Kick Shots

	Archer (6)	Reyes (9)	Combined
Planning	53.83	38.44	44.60
Executing	3.83	4.89	4.47
Total	57.67	43.33	49.07

Archer took over 15 seconds longer planning his kicks shots than Reyes. Reyes may have been guilty of playing a couple of kicks too quickly. In Game 17, for example, he took only nine seconds planning a kick before he scratched on the shot.

The Break

Reyes stuck with the same break position the whole match. Archer, in contrast, occasionally took some time deciding on his break spot. Archer consumed a little more than a second longer than Reyes in the execution phase, which often required several additional warm up strokes. Reyes' time is all about execution.

	Archer	**Reyes**
Execution (Ave.)	7.36	6.00
Longest Time	10.0	7.0
Shortest Time	6.0	5.0

Comparison of Time

The table below gives the combined totals for both players. The break clearly takes the most time to execute while kick shots are by far the most labor intensive in the planning phase.

Time for All Shots

	Preparation	**Execution**	**Total**
Break	-	6.71	6.71
Position Plays*	11.66	4.49	16.16
Safeties	28.00	4.85	32.85
Kick Shots	44.60	4.47	49.07

* Includes only those on game winning runouts.

Your Game: 10 Lessons on Time

The analysis in the sections on time leads us to the following 10 lessons:

1) The time you spend planning and executing a shot is an individual matter. Still, you want to avoid the extremes of playing too quickly or too slowly.

2) Take at least a couple of extra seconds in the execution phase of the break shot.

3) Get your planning done before you enter the execution phase of the shot cycle. Don't mix the two.

4) Identify the key shot(s) in a rack and take the time necessary to plan how you are going to deal with that shot.

5) When a position route or pattern is unclear, spend extra time in the planning phase of the cycle.

6) Spend at least 2-3 more seconds (but no more) in the execution phase of the shot cycle on difficult shots. And be sure to add at least a couple of warm up strokes to your routine.

7) Routine position plays should be played at a reasonably rapid clip as this enables you to play with rhythm. Again, this is a highly individual matter.

8) The time spent planning safeties depends on the complexity of the shot. Archer took from 10-99 seconds planning his safeties while Reyes took from 15-51 seconds.

9) Plan on spending the most time preparing for kick shots. Archer took from 30 to 74 seconds planning kick shots while Reyes range was 9-99 seconds.

10) Take notice of any changes in your pace of play in pressure situations, or have a friend do this for you. As a rule of thumb, it is better to take a little extra time to gather yourself for a pressure shot. A couple of deep breaths before shooting can work wonders. This is much better that hurrying to get the shot over with.

Your Game Summary
What You Can Learn From the Pros

Archer and Reyes excel in all facets of the game, as you might expect, considering they were the two top players in the world when this match was played. And yet, each exhibits minor weaknesses from time to time. This shows pool is a difficult game that can never be completely mastered. What largely separates top pros from the other players, however, is that their mistakes and weaknesses are kept to an absolute minimum.

Johnny Archer

Style Archer plays a very straightforward game. Archer shows there is no need to get fancy by complicating matters unnecessarily.

Fundamentals Archer's compact stroke is highly recommended. He changes the length of his bridge and stroke to match the requirements of the shot. He stays down over the ball exceptionally well.

Shotmaking   Archer is an excellent shotmaker, thanks largely to his excellent fundamentals.

Planning Archer is very meticulous as he takes exactly the amount of time he needs to plan a shot, no more, no less.

Execution Archer plays at a rapid pace on routine shots. On difficult shots he takes several more seconds in the execution phase of the shot cycle.

Safety Play Archer is a cagey defensive player as shown by his several excellent safeties. However he also failed to hook Reyes on a few chances because of errors in execution.

Kick Shots Archer takes plenty of time planning kick shots, which illustrates his methodical style of play. Archer's kicking game was brilliant when it needed to be in Game 21. He likes to use his cue as a measuring tool.

Rhythm Archer tends to play at a rapid clip on most shots. However, he slowed down measurably at the end of the match. A slower pace under pressure is better than rushing a shot and bypassing your normal routine.

Position and Patterns Archer has excellent speed and directional control. In addition, his patterns are very precise and on target in almost all cases.

The Break Archer consistently makes near perfect contact with the 1-ball while using a high powered break that's arguably the best in pool. Archer showed that he can win even without his break working because of his well-rounded game. Archer will quickly change positions when a spot is not producing results.

Efren Reyes

Style Reyes has a very relaxed style which helps reduce the pressure of big time pool. He seems to show the joy a child finds when playing a game for the love of the sport.

Fundamentals His stroke is long and relaxed thanks in part to his extremely light grip. Reyes, like Archer, stays down on his shots exceptionally well. He also has perhaps the fullest, straightest, and most relaxed follow through in pool. Reyes uses a very unusual set up technique with his tip often positioned well below the intended point of contact. The low tip gives him a good view of the cue ball, but causes him to occasionally apply excessive draw.

Shotmaking His brilliant shotmaking is due in part to his ability to hit the cue ball precisely where intended, which is underscored by his straight follow through, as mentioned above.

Planning Reyes spends little time in the planning phase on routine shots. He will take the necessary time plotting more difficult shots. However, there were a couple in instances where he seemed to shoot before conducting a complete appraisal of the shot.

Execution Reyes spends plenty of time in the execution phase as he follows a very well rehearsed routine that incorporates an average of nearly five warm up strokes per shot.

Safety Play Reyes' safety play was not particularly sharp in this match, in part because he was faced with several difficult safeties. As a rule, his cue ball control makes him a wizard on defense.

Kick Shots Reyes is the acknowledged master of the kicking game. He is out to accomplish a very strategic object on almost every kick shot. In addition, he has an uncanny ability to hit the portion of the ball he is aiming for.

Rhythm He spends less time planning than Archer, which indicates that he makes decisions quickly and confidently. Reyes is more into doing. He follows a very precise shooting routine, which includes a number of very well rehearsed warm-up strokes.

Position and Patterns His loose grip gives him a superb sense of feel when playing shape. However, his low tip position at address causes him to occasionally apply excessive draw. Reyes pattern play is generally superb, but he occasionally will choose a route that is open to debate.

The Break Reyes uses a slower speed than Archer which allows him to control the cue ball very well. His precise contact with the 1-ball gives him excellent results, especially if the table is receptive to a less powerful break, which is often the case.

A Quick Summary

Style Develop and learn your style and stick with it assuming, of course, that it works.

Fundamentals Stay relaxed in the transition, stay down, and follow through straight.

Shotmaking Play reasonably high percentage shots and look for safeties on the others.

Planning Take as much time as necessary to come up with the best shot, but don't make a point of spending so much time thinking that your execution suffers as a result.

Execution Follow a well rehearsed routine, but take a little more time on tough shots.

Safety Play Take ample time looking for the best safety. Consider which ball(s) needs the emphasis: the cue ball and/or the object ball.

Kick Shots Take the time to plan your route strategic objective, and make sure to at least make contact.

Rhythm Your pace of play is related to your knowledge of the game, your skill, and your natural tempo.

Position and Patterns Take the necessary time to decipher a layout. Learn to identify the primary emphasis in each position play (pocketing, speed, direction).

The Break In most but not all cases, you will want to use the most powerful break that enables you to still make solid contact with the 1-ball.

Your Game and The Pros

It is a most worthy goal to aspire to one day have the skills of an Archer or Reyes (or even a level somewhat close). However, while you are hopefully moving onwards and upwards with your game, you should learn to play your game while in competition. If that means mimicking the pros, fine. But in many situations you will find that your best strategy is to think like an amateur and do the things that are currently within your range of capabilities. In Game 16, for example I gave a situation where Archer went for a shot where an amateur might play a safety. The bottom line: know when you should or shouldn't copy a pro. In other words, know your strengths and weaknesses and play your game.

You Versus the Pros: A Test

After watching the pros run racks perhaps you are itching to get to the table. Rather than playing the game as always, why not try matching your skills to our superstars? You'll get some valuable practice and learn a lot about the current state of your position and pattern play. On the following page is a list of layouts that are diagrammed in the book.

Scoring

Set up the balls as closely as possible to the positions in each diagram. Each ball pocketed counts as a point. When you complete the run or miss, move on to the next game.

The number of shots played by Archer and Reyes totals 50 each. A perfect score is 100, the total number of balls in the 16 diagrammed runouts. A few of the diagrams start with the run already in progress, including Reyes' run in Game 16. The diagram on page 168 is taken from Game 11 and it is part of your exam.

Learn From Your Mistakes

As you progress through the runouts, take notice of your position play successes and failures. Then go back and watch the tape to see how the pro handled the situation. Also review the text that discusses the key shots in the layout and refer to *Play Your Best Nine Ball* as noted.

The Archer - Reyes Run Out Exam

Game	Page	Player	#Balls	Your Score
1	3	Archer	7	_____
2	7	Reyes	8	_____
3	11	Reyes	6	_____
4	15	Reyes	5	_____
5	21	Archer	6	_____
6	25	Reyes	7	_____
10	35	Reyes	6	_____
11	168	Archer	4	_____
13	43	Reyes	7	_____
14	47	Reyes	7	_____
15	51	Archer	6	_____
16	57	Reyes	4	_____
17	61	Archer	5	_____
18	65	Archer	8	_____
20	77	Archer	8	_____
21	89	Archer	6	_____
Total			**100**	_____

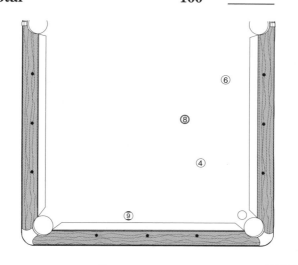

Analyzing Your Game

The Champions Checklist appeared in *Play Your Best Pool* and later was adapted for **PYBNB**.

The Champions Checklist

Fundamentals

__Grip
__Stance
__Bridge
__Stroke
__Aim
__Preshot routine

Basic Shotmaking

__Cut shots
__Thin cut shots
__Off the rail
__The long green
__Jacked up over a ball

Specialty Shots

__Banks - short rail
__Banks - long rail
__Caroms
__Billiards
__Combinations
__Curve shots

The Break

__Power break
__Control break
__Adaptability to the table

Kick Shots

__Basic routes
__Using english
__Using speed

Position Play

__Basics: stop, draw and follow
__No rail routes
__1-rail routes
__2 rail routes
__3 rail routes
__4 rail routes
__Use of outside english
__Use of inside english

Pattern Play

__Basic 3 ball patterns
__Advanced patterns

Safety Skills

__Full hit safeties
__Thin hit safeties
__Control of the cue ball
__Control of the object ball
__Knowledge of a variety of safeties
__Imagination

Push out

__Strategy
__Skills
__**The Lag for Break**

The checklist is a means of evaluating your game. You might also keep it handy during a viewing of the tape so you can conduct your own evaluation of our two champions in all critical areas of performance.

Appendices

Index
Video Analysis Lessons

The list below is your guide to the lessons that are appear throughout the main text. While there is great value in the written word, each lesson is reinforced by a demonstration on tape and by hearing the announcer's comments.

SloMo

There is nothing quite so revealing as running a tape in slow motion. Things begin to pop out at you that could never be seen at regular speed. The list below is just a sampling of some of the shots that are worth another look, either for their instructive value or for the pure pleasure of watching the balls do tricks in slow motion

Slow Motion Highlights (SloMo)

Patterns - Discussion Index

The pros executed several long runouts during the match largely due to their excellence in planning patterns. The list below and on the next page will take you to the discussion of patterns.

Announcer Index

Accu-Stats Videos

Pat Fleming

Pat Fleming, the founder of Accu-Stats, began recording matches on video in 1987. His goal was to dissect the matches and derive statistics for his Accu-Stats newsletter. Since then, he has blanketed the country recording events in Nine Ball, Straight Pool, One Pocket, Banks, and Three Cushion Billiards. In the process he has created a library of tapes that is an invaluable resource for fans and serious students of the game.

The Commentators

Bill Incardona is the voice of Accu-Stats, having logged far more hours in the booth than any other commentator. He gets psyched up for every match, and has an intensity that is completely genuine. He is extremely knowledgeable, has a great rapport with his guests, calls it like he's sees it and isn't afraid to ruffle a few feathers

Guests in the booth include some of the best players in the world. Among those I particularly enjoy are Grady Mathews, Nick Varner, Buddy Hall, Johnny Archer and Jim Rempe, Jay Helfert and Danny DiLiberto.

Recommended Matches

The Accu-Stats catalog lists over 300 videos of Nine Ball. The list below includes some of my favorites. Pat Fleming's favorites are marked with an asterisk (*). The list should help you to get started with building your collection. The commentators are listed below the players.

Battle of the Giants - 1993*
S17-05 Earl Strickland df. Mike Sigel 13-11
Bill Incardona, Mark Wilson $24 100 Min.
Straight Shooting Exhibition - 1993
189B-10 Mike Sigel df. Johnny Archer 11-10
Grady Mathews, Ed Sheahan $24 111 Min.
Reyes First U.S. Open Title-1994
199B-15 Efren Reyes df. Nick Varner 9-6
Bill Incardona, Johnny Archer $22 85 Min.
A Red Hot Finish - 1994*
S20-02 Francisco Bustamante df. E. Reyes 13-12
Grady Mathews, Buddy Hall $22 84 Min.
"The Magician" at Work - 1995
95PC-03 Efren Reyes df. Kim Davenport (F) 11-9
Nick Varner, Buddy Hall, Tom Kelly $24 71 Min.
The Shot Heard Around the Pool World- 1995*
S21-11 E. Reyes df. Earl Strickland (F)13-12
Bill Incardona, Jim Rempe $24 107 Min.
Run Out City - 1996
S23-10 Nick Varner df. Johnny Archer (F) 11-9
Bill Incardona, Buddy Hall $32 150 Min.
The Pearl on a Roll - 1997
229B-14 Earl Strickland df. E. Reyes (F) 11-3
Bill Incardona, Grady Mathews $20 65 Min.
Souquet's First Major Title in U.S. 1998*
S27-10 Ralf Souquet df. E. Reyes (F) 6-2,2-6,6-2
Bill Incardona, Jay Helfert $32 160 Min.
Hall Gets Out From Everywhere - 1998
239B15 Buddy Hall df. Tang Hoa (F) 11-5
Nick Varner, Kim Davenport $28 126 Min.
"The Pain, the Suffering" - 1998*
239B13 Mika Immonen df. Jim Rempe 11-10
Nick Varner, Jay Helfert $28 132 Min.

Archer Wins the U.S. Open - 1999
249B13 J. Archer df, Jeremy Jones (F) 11-7
Grady Mathews, Nick Varner $34   145 Min.
Reyes Captures The Masters - 2001
M1-14   Efren Reyes df. Earl Strickland   13-10
Grady Mathews, Buddy Hall $26   95 Min.

Player Review Favorites

These tapes feature an analysis by either or both of the contestants.
Jeanette Lee on Winning at Pool - 1994*
199B-13   Jeanette Lee df. Robin Dodson   11-3
Jeanette Lee, Pat Fleming $20   66 Min.
The Miz and Billy Show - 1994
199B-05   Steve Mizerak df. Earl Strickland   13-10
Steve Mizerak, Bill Incardona $24   91 Min.
Archer Talks Pool - 1997*
229B-05   Johnny Archer df. Ismael Paez   11-7
Johnny Archer, Grady Mathews $22   86 Min.

How to Order Pro Videos
Accu-Stats Video Productions
P.O. Box 299
Bloomingdale, NJ 07403

PH: 1-800-828-0397
E-mail: Accu-Stats@accu-stats.com
• Web: accu-stats.com
• Free Catalog - Lists 100's of tapes.
• Best and most popular tapes are highlighted in the catalog.
• Discounts for multiple purchases.

Phil Capelle

I've been continuously involved in pool in several capacities since I took up the game in early 1969. In 1995 I founded Billiards Press with the goal of providing students of the game with the finest instructional books on pool. *Play Your Best Pool* was published in late 1995. Since then I have written another four books with others projects in the planning stages. I continue to learn new things every day about this fascinating and challenging game of pool. In the years ahead, I look forward to sharing my findings with you, and I hope they greatly help your enjoyment of pool.

Books by Philip Capelle
BCA Certified Instructor
Columnist for *Pool & Billiard Magazine*

Play Your Best Pool
Your Complete Textbook on Pool
0-9649204-0-9   **$29.95** U.S. - **464 pages**
Contents:

Fundamentals	The Mental Game
Shotmaking	Competitive Play
How to Use English	How to Improve
Position Play	Practicing Pool
Eight Ball	How to Buy Equipment
Nine Ball	Appendix

Over <u>400</u> Illustrations

Play Your Best Nine Ball
Your Complete Guide to Nine Ball
0-9649204-3-3   **$29.95** U.S. - **480 pages**
Contents:

Shotmaking

The Break

Position Routes

Fine Points of Position

Principles of Position

Pattern Play

How to Run Out

Cluster Management

Reading the Table

Push Out Strategy

Safety Play

Kick Shots

The ABC's of Strategy

Competitive Nine Ball

Practicing Nine Ball

Appendix

Over <u>470</u> Illustrations

A Mind For Pool
How To Master the Mental Game
0-9649204-1-7   **$19.95** U.S. - **320 pages**
Contents:

Part One: Your Game

Part Two: Competition

Part Three: The Journey

What's Inside:

> **120** lessons on the mental game

> **80** lists for evaluating your game

> **295** of Capelle's Laws for Pool

> Over **500** great quotes

> Appendix

Play Your Best Straight Pool
A Complete Course on 14.1
Features a New Players Guide
0-9649204-2-5   **$24.95** U.S. - **416 pages**
Contents:

Position Play	Safety Play
Pattern Play	Strategy,
Secondary	Shotmaking
Break Shots	Learning to Play
Cluster Management	Straight Pool
Break Shots,	All About High Runs
How to Run a Rack	Appendix

<u>355</u> Illustrations

How To Order
To order direct, call
888-295-7665 or 714-894-1157
Order online www.billiardspress.com

Buy from Your Favorite Dealer
Books by Phil Capelle are also available at Billiard
supply stores and poolrooms.

Billiardspress.com
You are invited to visit our web site at the address
above. Below is the main table of the contents.
The Menu:

The Books	Video
Instruction	Capelle Research
Contests	Book Club
News and Views	Contact